I Want To Learn English

Level 1: For Beginners

by Jose V. Torres

IWTLE

Language Skills for the Real World

2nd Edition

This book belongs to _____

(Print your name here)

I Want To Learn English

By Jose V. Torres

This book is dedicated to my parents, Jesus Torres and Carlota Torres, who always wished to participate in English learning classes.

Audio tracks that accompany this textbook are available online on our website iwtle.com/2-2/audio2 or on Spotify.

To request CDs or tracks on USB, please email us at
iwanttolearnenglish3@gmail.com

ISBN-13: 979-8874453114

"Doctus cum libro."

SCOPE AND SEQUENCE

UNIT	OBJECTIVE	VOCABULARY	LISTENING AND SPEAKING
1 Greetings/Vowels (Pages 9-27)	Identify letters of the alphabet, vowels, and places around the city.	Numbers * Directions * Prepositions * Locations in the community	Greetings * Pronunciations of letters and vowels * Short conversations
2 Time/Digraphs (Pages 28-55)	Distinguish digraphs, tell time, and demonstrate comprehension of the verb "to be."	Words with digraphs * Pronouns * Sir/Ma'am * Thank you/You're welcome * Times of day	Polite requests and short conversations regarding the time * Asking/giving information using dates.
3 Calendar/Blends (Pages 56-93)	Properly identify and use ordinal numbers, dates on a calendar, and distinguish various jobs.	Words with consonant blends * Ordinal numbers * informal greetings * Days/Months * Jobs/Skills	Information about appointments, dates and times * Short conversations with dates
4 Money/Diphthongs (Pages 94-122)	Identify American currency, food, holidays, clothing types, colors, and safety signs.	Words with diphthongs * Coins/Dollar Bills * Holidays * Verbs with -ing * Foods * Safety Signs	Short conversations related to 'how much' and 'how many' * Listening activities related to safety

What activities are in the "Supplemental Activities" section?

Each of the four units within this book is comprised of Sections. Many Sections have subsections within them as well. Either at the start of a Section or throughout subsections, gaps in comprehension may occur related to the topics being covered in the Sections. For this reason, it was decided to include various "supplemental activities" to highlight, give additional practice, and provide opportunities for instructors to explore the nuances within the various themes. Students can also practice the skills and materials being covered in the Sections and subsections. The supplemental activities do not have audio components corresponding with them. They are to be used at the instructor's discretion. They provide insight into how much students truly understand about the topics. With this in mind, the instructor can decide to delve deeper into the subjects based on students' needs or move on to the next Section.

GRAMMAR	READING AND WRITING	CONTEXTUALIZATION AND LIFE SKILLS	CASAS AND EFF STANDARDS (♦)
Spelling * Prepositional phrases	Spelling * Completing sentences with missing words * Identifying true or false	Express understanding of directions * Identifying common locations in the community	0.1.1, 0.1.2, 0.1.4, 0.2.1, 1.2.6, 2.2.5, 4.6.1, 6.0.1, 6.0.2 ♦ Speak so others understand ♦ Listen actively
Use of subject pronouns * The verb "to be" * Simple present tense * Using a/an * Preposition of time	Proper sentence order * Identifying the correct times of day * Sentences using contractions	Calculating hours worked * Employee time sheet * Asking and giving information about time	0.1.8, 2.3.1, 2.3.2, 2.3.4, 4.1.2, 4.2.1, 6.1.1 ♦ Speak so others understand ♦ Cooperate with others ♦ Listen actively
Future tense using "will" * Using can/can't * Use of should/shouldn't	Identifying qualifications in job advertisements * Reading and writing about job descriptions	Properly completing a job application * Job Search * Making / Canceling appointments	1.2.1, 3.1.2, 4.1.3, 4.1.6, 4.1.8, 4.5.1 ♦ Find and get a job ♦ Convey ideas in writing ♦ Read with understanding ♦ Listen actively
Use of how much and how many * Present Progressive Tense	Identifying holidays * Writing about holidays in home countries * Descriptive sentences	Counting money * Understanding quantities * Recognizing various safety signs	1.1.6, 1.2.1, 1.2.4, 1.6.1, 1.2.6, 1.2.8, 1.2.9, 2.7.1, 3.4.2, 3.5.2, 4.3.1, 4.3.3 ♦ Solve problems and make decisions ♦ Observe critically

What activities are in the "Assessments" section?

Each of the four units within this book has a phonetic component. For example, Unit 1 focuses on vowels. There are four vowel assessments (i.e., one pre-assessment and three actual assessments). The vowel assessments in Unit 1 are scored and those scores logged in order to track students' abilities to discriminate the various vowel sounds in words -both when they are heard and articulated. What the data in the trials of this text book has shown is students who demonstrate gains in their phonetic awareness generally show gains on their CASAS exams (and other exit exams) at the end of the course. The assessments in Units 2-4 are mainly for the instructor to continue checking the progress of students' general phonetic awareness. These components include digraphs, consonant blends and diphthongs. It is strongly suggested scores for these assessments be logged by the instructor to track students' progress. Tracking sheets are available in the teacher's edition and online at www.iwtle.com.

To the instructors

This textbook was designed using a concept I call "***swing differentiation***." As an instructor for many years working with adult English Language Learners, it has always been challenging to supplement textbooks used in class –usually skimming through various other textbooks and fishing through websites all over the Internet. One reason is, in truth, textbooks are generally rigid and target specific details. Or they jump from topic to topic seemingly at random. So it is absolutely necessary to supplement lessons pulled from a   standard textbook to cover broad topics. This textbook was developed to be more flexible than standard issued books. It has components within every unit which incorporate differentiation inherently. It comes with practical activities, worksheets, information pages, audio components, and puzzles designed to engage every student at the beginner level with real purpose.

What is *Swing Differentiation*?

The idea behind *swing differentiation* is familiar. As ELA instructors, differentiation is at the heart of what we constantly do in the classroom. In truth, at its core, differentiation entails students at multiple levels receive activities and given instruction in accordance with their levels. Essentially, students who are at a higher   proficiency level, let's say, should be engaged in activities challenging and rigorous to them, while those at a lower proficiency level can also be engaged but not be overwhelmed. Somehow, students at all levels should make gains in the objective of the lesson in spite of their proficiency gaps. Obviously, this is challenging and time consuming in terms of planning. *Swing differentiation* resolves some critical problems in this scenario. First, there is an "umbrella" goal for all students within a class, even those with students at multiple levels (though there are limits to these multiple level and I will go into this later). What instructors need to remember is students who are "beginners" all come with the same desires:

1)   They want to speak English better

2)   They want to understand English better when it is spoken to them

3)   They want to use what they already know and communicate it using English

These goals are very basic and central to why a student even enters an ELA classroom in the first place. It's what they truly want. The issue, of course, is how to efficiently manage the time allotted for class so students can get the most out of the instruction you provide. Often when instructors differentiate lessons, they make some aspects of the lesson more challenging for those at higher levels and dilute it for those at lower levels. S*wing differentiation* eliminates this segregation of instruction. Keep in mind English Learners generally need stronger phonemic awareness, and their gaps in comprehension is largely attributed to this.

Swing differentiation in this textbook means differentiated activities are already embedded in the lessons for instructors to use at the appropriate time. If an activity is "easy for a group of students," then just swing up to the next Section or subsection. This textbook is designed to accommodate students who need more in-depth focuses on phonemic or grammatical components by giving instructors the tools to stay on a subject, topic, Section or activity as long as necessary before moving to the next Section. In more practical terms, the book works like this: set a goal, build a scaffold to get there in tiered steps, and take all students there simultaneously. Students who enter a beginner ELA class clearly have many of the same difficulties.

As stated, these difficulties are rooted in their phonemic awareness. For example, all beginners likely cannot distinguish the long and short vowels. This is where *I Want To Learn English* begins. With the thousands of students I've taught at the beginning level over the years, none of them were able to make this distinction on the first day. Most had trouble correctly pronouncing each letter of the alphabet, and many could not even accurately phonetically spell their own names. What does this mean? It means before these students can get a better grasp of the English language and all its complexities, they need to first master the very basics of it, and that means knowing the letters, the sounds they produce, and vowels. Once students master this, then they can expand their comprehension of word structures, read better, articulate more fluidly, and put together phrases and coherent sentences. Even though initial tests indicated my students were at multiple levels, they clearly needed the fundamentals of the language before they could truly understand and retain meaning from common themes such as community locations (prepositions), giving and receiving directions, expressing themselves (likes/dislikes, etc.), and deriving basic (but critical) information from short conversations. Many visuals are needed to help students get the general concepts, and their prior knowledge helps them make the connections. Since students generally assemble in a class at multiple levels, the activities within the units accommodate this. For example, in unit one, once students get a better understanding of letters and vowels, they begin short greeting conversations. Those students at the lowest levels could work on the most basic greeting conversation with a partner. However, there is another conversation which is designed to challenge students and demonstrate their understanding of tenses (differentiated activities are in red throughout the textbook). Instructors need to pay close attention to how students engage in this swing conversation because if it is too difficult for them to comprehend, then perhaps it would be best to step back and reiterate the overall concept. (As a side note, I have asked students if they do not want to try the swing conversation for fear it is too difficult and could be skipped, but not a single student has ever declined the challenge.)

Deep dive activities in the book.

Throughout the textbook, there are Sections and subsections. Deep dive activities are always in subsections. A Section is a whole number. For example, *3*. A subsection would be a decimal. For example, *3.1*. (More on the structure of Sections and subsections a little later.) Just remember if you see an activity in red, it is loaded with concepts, vocabulary, or cultural nuances relevant to the subject in the Section. These afford opportunities for instructors to expand on the topics and allow students to explore the details of the subject matter. As you progress through the book, subjects will present many instances when greater expansion of a topic can be brought into a discussion or whole group explanation. Of course, instructors could elect to not proceed with differentiated activities if they believe it is too difficult for their students.

Are there "fun activities" in this book?

I cannot overemphasize the point students are in an ELA class for serious reasons. Generally, this is a business for them (i.e., it is important for them to communicate better in English for work, school, in the community, etc.). It is not a game by any stretch. That is why there are no games in this textbook. I don't discourage the use of games and certainly there are many instructors who incorporate games and game-like activities in their lessons, but there are none in this text book. Instead, I've included humor, puns, and comical situations students can relate to. For example, there is a reoccurring character that appears throughout the book. His name is Sam. This gentleman makes some quirky remarks, and pursues (unsuccessfully) the attention of a young woman named Eva. Sam's reluctance to "give up" no matter how the odds are stacked is a motif for the challenges ELA students face with their English studies. In spite of how *"hot sauce"* gives him stomach problems or Eva's reluctance to go to lunch with him, Sam's perseverance to the end does eventually pay off. This is an undercurrent theme instructors could "play" with throughout the lessons in this textbook. It is not blazingly obvious, but I made it that way so students could get creative and invent a back story for Sam and the little tidbits of his life we find in the Sections.

Contextualizing and Building Students' Language Skills

The essential language skills are emphasized throughout this textbook. They include listening, speaking, reading and writing. All of these skills require a degree of decoding. This begins at the phonemic level. It is important for instructors to spend a little time becoming familiar with the focus of the Sections in each unit. There are opportunities to formulate whole group activities from the Sections and the activities already in place. There are many listening activities, some comprehensive, others contextualize conversations and clarify pronunciations. Many activities call for peer to peer reading exercises, practice phrases and responses, and some specific conversation starters. These are designed to challenge students to engage each other in discussing relevant topics ranging from job related language to functions in the community.

Comprehension Checks and Unit Assessments

Each unit comes with a "Comprehension Check" somewhere in the middle of the unit for instructors to gauge how well students are understanding the content. Use the data from these to determine whether you should revisit the subject matters covered thus far in the unit or proceed. Unit Assessments mimic standardized assessments, but go farther into just how much students understand the content. This information gives instructors a real window into students' skills and the gains they are making. In some ways, the unit assessments are more challenging than standardized tests because they measure students' movements in the Blooms Taxonomy model (*Knowledge* to *Comprehension* to *Application* and *Analysis*), rather than just basic comprehension. This textbook is designed to surpass the expectations of any standardized test and literally prepare them for the community at large.

How does this book work with multiple levels?

Instructors generally encounter in classes with students at multiple proficiency levels a certain frustration in differentiating appropriate activities for the whole class. As long as students are within the low beginner and low intermediate levels, this textbook has many practical uses. This is because it centers around the phonetic foundation of the English language and is designed to help students gain a stronger phonemic awareness in order to understand basic communication essentials. Students on the higher intermediate and advanced levels do not struggle with this as much. They already have a strong phonemic awareness, and thus would not necessarily need many of the skills targeted by the lessons in this textbook. This does not mean they cannot gain anything by using it. In fact, some students at the higher intermediate level have used this textbook in the trials and responded extremely positive when asked what they gained from it. The difference is in the grammar. High intermediate level students often need more grammatical structure understanding of the language in order to make greater steps forward. For that, a second level of *I Want To Learn English* will be developed in the near future. For the record, this textbook is best used with students at the low and high beginner levels.

Sections and Subsections

Although there are four distinct units in this textbook, the overall structure is based on *Sections*. There are 51 Sections in this textbook that transcend the units. This is at the heart of *swing differentiation*. Instructors can plan their lessons in the order of the book because it is structured in the order of the crucial needs students have at the beginner level. There is nothing random about the order of the Sections. If instructors find their students do not need to cover extensively, say, "prepositions," then they can proceed to the next set of Sections. However, if students have a good understanding of prepositions, then they shouldn't be beginners in the first place. What instructors need to understand before they decide to "jump ahead" or "jump around" the Sections in this book is years of research went into finding the best order of lessons beginners need to understand. For example, most beginner textbooks start with the alphabet. Why? Because beginners generally have difficulty with letters, their sounds, how to spell, etc. That is about the only thing this textbook has in common with mainstream books. The rest are strategically ordered lessons, moving to vowels and then numbers. This is because numbers are generally understood and with the frustration of letters and vowels, students find elation in numbers (something they generally understand no matter what their native language is). Topics move from Section to Section in the best order determined by the years of trials.

Subsections are expansions of Sections. For example, Section 19 deals with time. It goes on to 19.1, 19.2, all the way to 19.7. Each of the subsections is related to time. The swing differentiation activities begin at 19.3. Here is where the challenging aspects of the book really make students think on more critical levels. It is essential to understand that students should not try 19.4, for example, if they don't grasp the information in 19.3. This is how the book is structured from start to finish. For this reason, I recommend instructors start with Section 1 and go in sequential order until they reach 51 or get as far as they can within the time restrictions of the course.

Listening Components

Many of the Sections and subsections have listening components. One of the things to keep in mind when using these listening tools is the "real" nature about them. I deliberately used "regular," every day people to model the conversations and provide the listening activities for students to decipher. I elected not to hire "professional" voice actors or radio personalities for this because when students use their skills in the real world, they will encounter "real" people and not radio voice actors. I believe this presents a whole other set of challenges for students. They have to not only discriminate all the words, the sounds, and cultural nuances, but also accents (regional, ethnic and second language), volume levels, intonation variations, monotone speech, and other real world elements. Much of the voice product was made by me (the author), but selected people participated to convey a variety of situations without making the audio tracks sound homogenized. In all of the trials, students found the variety of voices to be more "authentic" to what they find on a day to day basis and reinforced the need to pay closer attention to details.

Video Components and QR Codes

The first edition of this book had great success because so much of the textbook can be used outside of the classroom with the use of audio components. However, with a vast majority of students using social media apps, it was advantageous to incorporate video components to align with the activities with the lessons to further enhance the learning experience. Most of the activities within this textbook have a video component that aligns with it (including the first two Comprehension Checks) and those activities have a QR code on the pages to make finding those videos easier. Instructors can now assign practice activities and students can access them easily using their smart phones.

Exclusion of the Past Tense

The three tenses highlighted in this textbook are the simple present, the future (using "will"), and the present progressive (continuous). I left out the past tense because it is a subject that should be explored more at the intermediate levels. The three mentioned tenses have some universal rules that low beginner students can digest with some relative comprehension. However, the past tense is far too complex with various forms of conjugated verbs that would take a number of Sections to cover and at the beginner level, it may ultimately confuse students more than help. Essentially, in my professional opinion, students at the beginning level need more understanding of the phonetic composition and general mechanics of English before venturing into a subject as gray as the past tense. This is why, in Section 11.1, the first line in the dialogue "I walked around for hours" will raise many questions from students. The inclusion of this line is deliberate. Instructors should not go into a grand explanation of the past tense. I do not cover this later in the book and put that line there specifically to show how complex of an issue the past tense presents at this level. Instead, focus on Pat's humor in addressing Sam's concern about getting an upset stomach if he eats too much hot sauce. Also, keep in mind if random appearances of the past tense sprout up throughout this book, it was likely unavoidable. Instructors can always tell students that the past tense will be covered later at another level.

For updates and more information, answer keys, and corresponding audio tracks (and videos), please visit iwtle.com/2-2/audio2.

This second edition features QR codes to videos on our official I Want To Learn English YouTube channel, which are associated with particular lessons and activities throughout the textbook.

Subscribe at YouTube.com/JoseTorresiwtle.

I Want To Learn English

UNIT 1

GREETINGS.
LET'S GET STARTED.

In this section, we will cover:

*Basic Greetings/Conversations
*Alphabet, Vowels, Intro to Numbers
*Community Vocabulary Words
*Simple Present Tense
* Prepositions of Place
* Directions
* True and False

Hello!

SOUNDING OUT LETTERS

PHONICS

▶ (Play Track 1)

1. Let's begin with the English alphabet. Look at each letter as you hear it spoken. Repeat each letter as you hear them.

A a	B b	C c	D d
E e	F f	G g	H h
I i	J j	K k	L l
M m	N n	O o	P p
Q q	R r	S s	T t
U u	V v	W w	X x
Y y	Z z		

Supplemental component p. 138-139

2. The letters **A E I O U** are called *vowels*. Vowels produce two sounds. One is called *long vowels* and the other is called *short vowels*. Listen and repeat both long and short vowels.

▶ (Play Track 2)

A	E	I	O	U

PRACTICE NUMBERS

 (Play Track 3)

3. Let's continue with numbers. Repeat each number as you hear it spoken.

0	1	2	3	4	5	6	7	8	9	10
11	12	13	14	15	16	17	18	19	20	21

3.1 *Now, try larger numbers.*

30	40	50	60	70	80	90	100	200	300
400	500	600	700	800	900	1,000	10,000	100,000	1,000,000

Supplemental component p. 140

 (Play Track 4)

3.2 Now, practice pronouncing the numbers and spelling them from 1-20. Then 30-100.

0 - Zero

1- One

2 - Two

3 - Three

4 - Four

5 - Five

6 - Six

7 - Seven

8 - Eight

9 - Nine

10 - Ten

11 - Eleven

12 - Twelve

13 - Thirteen

14 - Fourteen

15 - Fifteen

16 - Sixteen

17 - Seventeen

18 - Eighteen

19 - Nineteen

20 - Twenty

30 - Thirty

40 - Forty

50 - Fifty

60 - Sixty

70 - Seventy

80 - Eighty

90 - Ninety

100 - One hundred

Supplemental component p. 141

MORE NUMBERS

Practice pronouncing the numbers with our YouTube video. Use your phone camera and click the link to the QR code.

3.3

Student Challenge: Practice numbers from 200-1,000,000.

 (Play Track 5)

200 - Two hundred	2,000 - Two thousand
300 - Three hundred	3,000 - Three thousand
400 - Four hundred	4,000 - Four thousand
500 - Five hundred	5,000 - Five thousand
600 - Six hundred	10,000 - Ten thousand
700 - Seven hundred	100,000 - One hundred thousand
800 - Eight hundred	1,000,000 - One Million
900 - Nine hundred	
1,000 - One thousand	

LEARN VOCABULARY BASICS: DIRECTIONS

 (Play Track 6)

4. Listen to the words and repeat.

1. Listen	4. Write	7. Spell
2. Repeat	5. Look	8. Match
3. Talk	6. Point	

You **listen** with your ears.

When you **repeat**, you say something again.

You **talk** with your mouth.

You **write** with your hands.

You **look** with your eyes.

You **point** with your finger.

You **spell** using letters.

You **match** two things that are the same.

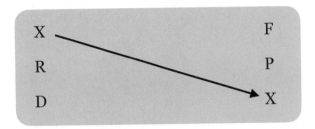

I.   You will see "**listen and repeat**" many times. This means when you hear something spoken, you will say it again.

        Example: **Listen and repeat:**   *My name is Jose.*

                                                          Tomorrow is Tuesday.

II. When directions say "**talk**," this means you speak to others.

        Example: ***Talk to your partner about your job.***

III. When you see the direction "**write**," use a pen or pencil to spell out the words in a sentence.

   Write your name.

   _____

IV. The word "**look**" means you focus on only one thing. When you "**point**," you use your fingers.

   Example: Look at the man with the hat and point at him.

V. You "**spell**" words using letters.

   Example: ***Name is Jose. J-O-S-E.***

VI. You "**match**" things that are the same or go together using a line.

   Computer

   Car

   Candy

CHECK YOUR SKILLS: DIRECTIONS

4.1 Match the vocabulary words with the pictures.

1. Listen	4. Repeat	7. Spell
2. Write	5. Look	8. Match
3. Talk	6. Point	

4.2

In the English alphabet, you have uppercase and lowercase letters (see section 1). Uppercase letters are known as "capital" letters are the larger of the two. They are primarily used at the beginning of sentences, proper nouns and abbreviations.

Names of people and places are always capitalized (using uppercase letters). Look at the examples.

USA	**Las Vegas**	**Miami**	**Nancy**	**I**	**Texas**

Below is a list of cities in America. Write them using capital letters. The first one is completed for you.

1. boston   _____ Boston _____

2. dallas   _____

3. fresno   _____

4. tulsa   _____

5. atlanta   _____

6. indianapolis   _____

7. grand rapids   _____

8. orlando   _____

9. santa ana   _____

10. phoenix   _____

11. jacksonville   _____

12. yuma   _____

WHAT IS YOUR NAME?  (Play Track 7)

5. Listen to the recording. Then, practice the short greeting and the spelling of **_your_** name.

Supplemental component p. 142

> A: Hello. My name is Bella.
> B: Nice to meet you. I am Schuyler.
> A: How do you spell that?
> B: S-C-H-U-Y-L-E-R.

Student 1: Hello. My name is
_____.
Student 2: Nice to meet you.
I am _____.
Student 1: How do you spell
your name?
Student 1: _____.

 (Play Track 8)

6. Look at the short greeting dialogue. Listen to the recording and then repeat. Then, practice with a partner.

John: Hello. I am John.
Mary: Hello, John. I am Mary.
John: Nice to meet you, Mary.
Mary: Same here. Nice to meet you, too.

6.1 _Student Challenge: Listen and repeat. Practice the conversation with a partner._

 (Play Track 9)

John: Mary, where is Ray?
Mary: Oh, Ray? He is home.
John: Will he be here tomorrow?
Mary: Yes, he will be here tomorrow.

VOWELS AND NEW VOCABULARY WORDS

 (Play Track 10)

7. Let's review the vowels: A E I O U

Practice saying the following words that have the long and short vowels.

| / ā / able | / ē / read | / ī / ice cream | / ō / boat | / ū / United States |

EXAMPLES USING SHORT VOWELS

/ ă /		apple
/ ĕ /		eggs
/ ĭ /		sit
/ ŏ /		pot
/ ŭ /		cup

Take the long and short vowel quiz. Use your smart phone camera on the QR code and play the video to test your vowel skills.

The direct link to the vowel quiz video is:

https://bit.ly/3ME7yXA

You can also visit the I Want To Learn YouTube channel:

YouTube.com/JoseTorresiwtle

Now, practice saying the long and short vowels on your own. Use the example words to help you.

CAPITALIZATION PRACTICE

7.1 Capitalize every word in a person's name. For example:

Michael Quinn   Edward Snow   Dan Murphy   Thelma Green   Nia Ruiz

Rewrite the following names using capital letters.

1. picabo street _____

2. david roads _____

3. george washington _____

4. serena williams _____

5. neil armstrong _____

6. henry ford _____

7. mary-kate olsen _____

8. albert collins _____

9. margaret thatcher _____

10. marie antoinette _____

Capitalize the middle initial of a person's name. For example:

Jose V. Torres   Billy D. Williams   John D. Rockefeller   Johnny B. Goode

Rewrite the following names using capital letters.

1. michael j. fox _____

2. george w. bush _____

3. john f. kennedy _____

4. j. k. rowling _____

VOWELS AND NEW VOCABULARY WORDS

 (Play Track 11)

8. Practice pronunciation: Short Vowel / o /.

Car	Far	Crosswalk	Park
Stoplight	Mailbox	Parking Lot	Post Office

Practice pronunciation: Long Vowel / e /.

Street	Library	Building	Flea Market

Practice the pronunciation of some more location words. Listen and mark where you hear the short vowel / o / or long vowel / e /.

1. Check cashing store
2. Bank
3. Lawyers office
4. Mechanic shop
5. Clinic

6. Pharmacy
7. Hospital
8. Church
9. Electronic store
10. Gas station

11. Restaurant
12. Dentist
13. Supermarket
14. Convenience store
15. Police station

Supplemental Component p. 143-144

OTHER VOCABULARY WORDS

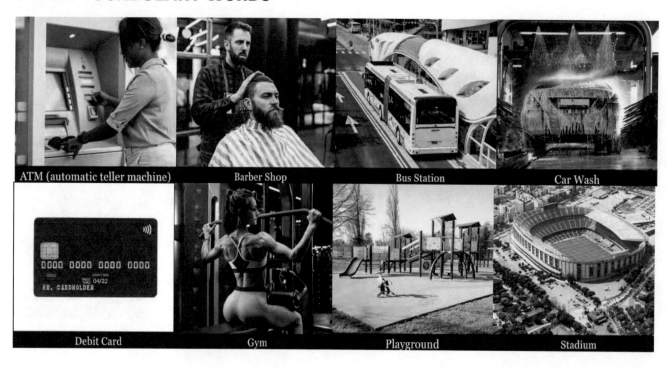

ATM (automatic teller machine)

Barber Shop

Bus Station

Car Wash

Debit Card

Gym

Playground

Stadium

9. Practice matching the clues with the vocabulary words.

AROUND THE CITY CROSSWORD PUZZLE

Across

1. where you buy medicine

4. where you buy food for the week

5. where you sit down and order food

6. person who fixes your teeth

7. where you go when you get sick

Down

2. a place of worship

3. where you buy gas for your car

 (Play Track 12)

9.1 Listen to the short conversations and answer the questions.
(There may be more than one answer.)

1. Where does Margaret need to go? _____

2. Where should Luis take his car? _____

3. Where does the man need to go? _____

4. Where should the man go for a new computer?_____

5. Where should Mario go? _____

AROUND THE CITY: LOCATIONS AND DIRECTIONS

10. Listen and repeat the words and phrases.

 (Play Track 13)

on	between	across from
next to	on the corner of	in back of
behind	in front of	near

Look at the map and answer the questions that follow using the prepositions.

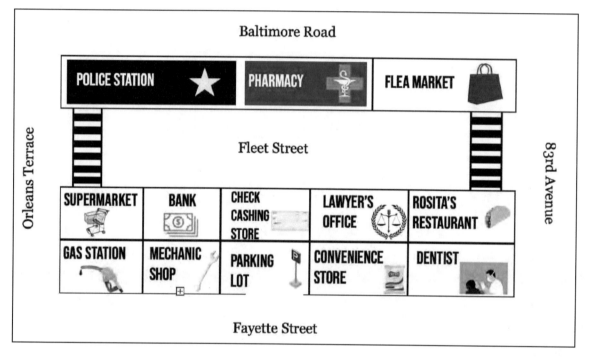

1. The police station is _____ the supermarket.

2. The dentist is _____ 83rd Avenue and Fayette Street.

3. The _____ is between the police station and the flea market.

4. The convenience store is on _____ street.

5. The gas station is _____ the supermarket.

6. There is a crosswalk _____ the supermarket.

7. Where is the check cashing store? _____

Supplemental Component p. 145-148

DO YOU UNDERSTAND?

▶ (Play Track 14)

10.1 Look at the map in Section 10 and listen to the statements.

First, let's do number 1 together. Listen and answer the questions by circling either A, B, or C.

1.   A   (B)   C

Now, let's try a few more.

2.   A   B   C

3.   A   B   C

4.   A   B   C

Now, let's try some on your own. Listen carefully. You'll hear everything two times.

5.   A   B   C

6.   A   B   C

7.   A   B   C

Listen and answer the following questions on the lines.

8. _____

9. _____

10. _____

AROUND THE CITY:
UNDERSTANDING LOCATIONS AND DIRECTIONS

 (Play Track 15)

11. Listen and read the short conversation. Then, practice with a partner.

Sam: Do you know where the flea market is?

Pat: Yes. It is on the corner of Fleet Street and

83rd Avenue.

Sam: Do you think it is open now?

Pat: Maybe, but I am not positive.

11.1 Listen to the conversation and then practice with a partner.

 (Play Track 16)

Sam: I walked around for hours. I am very hungry now.

Pat: There is a good restaurant across from the pharmacy and the flea market.

Sam: What kind of restaurant is it?

Pat: It's a Mexican restaurant. I love their tacos, especially with hot sauce.

Sam: Hot Sauce! Oh, too much hot sauce and I will have stomach problems.

Pat: Like I said, the pharmacy is across the street.

WRITING PRACTICE: PUNCTUATION

11.2 When you write a sentence, it always ends with a punctuation mark. For example, a sentence always ends with a period, which looks like a small dot [.]. A question always ends with a questions mark [?]. Excited statements end with an exclamation point [!]. Look at the example below.

Mario is from Mexico.

> There are two important things to notice in this sentence. Capitalization of the names and the period at the end.

Look at the sentences below. Rewrite them with the correct capitalization and punctuation. The first one is done for you.

1. mary if from canada   <u>Mary is from Canada.</u>

2. juan is from guatemala   _____

3. i am from el salvador   _____

4. they are students   _____

5. we are chinese   _____

6. i live in richmond   _____

Now, write three sentences about yourself. Remember to capitalize and punctuate. For example, *"My name is Jose."*

1. _____

2. _____

3. _____

TRUE OR FALSE?

11.3   Write "T" if the statement is *true*, or "F" if the statement is *false*.

For example:

___T___ Washington, D.C. is in the United States.

___F___ This is a dog.

Write "T" in the line if the answer is TRUE. Write "F" on the line if the answer is FALSE.

 _____ 1. This is a pencil.

 _____ 4. This is a camera.

 _____ 2. This is a cat.

 _____ 5. This is a ball.

 _____ 3. This is a chair.

 _____ 6. This is a table.

11.4 Test your skills by practicing more true/false questions.

1. _____ You **listen** with your ears.

2. _____ You **talk** with your eyes.

3. _____ "Cat" has a short / e / sound.

4. _____ You buy medicine at the pharmacy.

5. _____ You buy food at the supermarket.

6. _____ There's a crosswalk in the bank.

7. _____ Dogs have four legs.

8. _____ You **write** with your hands.

9. _____ Rabbits eat spaghetti.

MORE PRACTICE ON OUR YOUTUBE CHANNEL. USE THE QR CODE AND PRACTICE ALONG WITH THE VIDEO.

12. UNIT 1 ASSESSMENT

Part 1:

Look again at the map in Section 10. Check each of the following statements and write either "T" for true or "F" for false.

_____ 1. The check cashing store is across from the supermarket.

_____ 2. The convenience store is between the parking lot and the dentist.

_____ 3. Rosita's Restaurant is on the corner of 83rd Ave. and Fayette Street.

_____ 4. The gas station is on the corner of Orleans Terrace and Fayette Street.

_____ 5. The lawyer's office is across from the flea market.

Part 2:

 (Play Track 17)

Listen to the conversations. Listen again and answer the following questions.

Drill One

1. What is the man looking for?
2. How far away is the man?
3. What street is the man on?

Drill Two

4. What is the woman looking for?
5. On what street is the lawyer's office on?
6. What is the lawyer's office next to?

Around The City:
      Listening Drills 1 and 2

Circle the best answer to the questions.
For example: A   B   Ⓒ

        1. A   B   C

        2. A   B   C

        3. A   B   C

        4. A   B   C

        5. A   B   C

        6. A   B   C

UNIT 2
TIME AND DIGRAPHS

In this section, we will cover:
- *Digraphs*
- *Verb "To Be" (is, are, am)*
- *Telling Time*
- *Days, Months, Seasons*

Digital clock

Analog clock

 DIGRAPHS

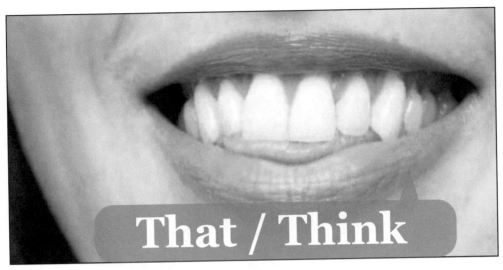

That / Think

13. Let's begin with practicing the pronunciations of digraphs. Listen and repeat.

 (Play Track 18)

Digraph	Sounds Like	Example
th	*th*	three
sh	*sh*	shoe
ch	*ch*	chicken
ph	*f*	phone
ng	*ing*	sing
wh	*w*	when

14. Look at the pictures and practice saying the words.

 (Play Track 19)   Supplemental component p. 149

Whale

13
Thirteen

Check

Chair

Shoe

These girls

Phone

Ring

- -

15. Point to the words that have digraphs and practice by repeating them.

 (Play Track 20)

Chip   What   Hat   Graph

Think   Wheel   Ship   Hot

Thing   Sit   Long   There

Supplemental Component p. 149

PRACTICE PRONUNCIATION

 (Play Track 21)

16. Listen and repeat the following numbers. Focus on the digraph "TH."

3	13	30	31	32
three	thirteen	thirty	thirty-one	thirty-two
33	**34**	**35**	**36**	**37**
thirty-three	thirty-four	thirty-five	thirty-six	thirty-seven
38	**39**	**43**	**300**	**333**
thirty-eight	thirty-nine	forty-three	three hundred	three hundred thirty-three

16.1. Practice pronunciations of more numbers. Click the QR code to practice along with a video. The numbers all have the voiceless "TH" digraph.

3 - Three	36 - Thirty-six
13 - Thirteen	37 - Thirty-seven
23 - Twenty-three	38 - Thirty-eight
30 - Thirty	39 - Thirty-nine
31 - Thirty-one	43 - Forty-three
32 - Thirty-two	53 - Fifty-three
33 - Thirty-three	63 - Sixty-three
34 - Thirty-four	73 - Seventy-three
35 - Thirty-five	83 - Eighty-three

Practice with video! Use QR code above.

33

16.2 Listen to the sentences and repeat. Focus on the digraphs.

 (Play Track 22)

1. Heather is from Philadelphia.

2. She is a math teacher.

3. Charley and Sharon are students.

Simple Present Tense

16.3 Practice the Conversation. Focus on the digraphs.

 (Play Track 23)

Phillip: Hi, Thelma. Who is Chuck?

Thelma: Oh, Chuck is the new doctor from Washington.

Phillip: He's from Washington?

Thelma: Yes. One more doctor is coming from Richmond.

Phillip: We have thirty-two doctors. One more makes thirty-three.

Thelma: That's right.

Phillip: How many doctors are in the hospital?

Thelma: There are three hundred thirty-three.

Phillip: Wow. Thank you for that information, Thelma.

Thelma: You're welcome.

Supplemental Component p. 150

17. WHAT ARE PRONOUNS?

Pronouns are used in the place of nouns, usually names of people, places or just common things. For example, John is a man. The pronoun "he" can be used in the place of John. So you can say "John is my friend. He is from California." For a female, you use the pronoun "she." For more than one person, you use "they." All other things you use "it."

Look at the examples below:

Name	Pronoun
Manuel	he
Rosa	she
John and Sam	they
Tom and I	we
chair	it
(when talking about yourself)	I

Hello. I am John.
I am from Los Angeles.

This is Sofia and Alfonso.
They are from Portugal.

Claudette is a student.
She is from Jamaica.

I am Jake and that is Mike.

We play professional soccer.

Thomas is a model.
He lives in New York.

My name is Jing.
I live in California.

The watch is nice.
It is expensive.

17.1 Subject pronouns take the place of nouns and are generally placed before a verb, Especially the verb "to be." For example:

John is a student.   **He** is a student.
Martha is my wife.   **She** is my wife.
The bird is in the tree.   **It** is in the tree.

Look at the nouns. Fill in the blanks using the pronouns **he, she**, *it, we* or **they**.

Nouns	Pronouns
Mary	
Thomas	
book	
Manuel and I	
dog and cat	
brother	
mother	
Beth and Phillip	
cheese	
sunshine	
Adesh and Pat	
soda	
sister	
Thelma and I	
tree	
George Washington	
The lawyers	
Mrs. White	
My family and I	

SIMPLE PRESENT TENSE: THE VERB "TO BE"

18. The simple present tense uses the verbs is, are, and am. Use "is" for singular subject Nouns, "are" for plural subject nouns and "am" only when using "I."

Remember: singular = 1 noun   plural = 2 or more nouns

Look at the examples below.

Using "is" (Singular)

She <u>is</u> from Sweden.

He <u>is</u> (a) student. ⟶ The use of the article "a" tells you the noun is ***singular***.

It <u>is</u> between the pencil and the book.

Using "are" (Plural)

We <u>are</u> in class.

They <u>are</u> my friends.

John and Pedro <u>are</u> brothers. ⟶ Multiple people or things are ***plural*** nouns.

Mary and I <u>are</u> next to the door.

Using "am" (Only with "I")

I <u>am</u> from Miami.

I <u>am</u> on the crosswalk.

I <u>am</u> a student.

18.1 Complete the following sentences using ***is***, ***are***, or ***am***.

1. Chen _____ a student from China.

2. I _____ in class.

3. They _____ brothers.

4. Athena and I _____ friends.

5. It _____ next to the table.

6. We _____ in the United States.

7. Whitney _____ my sister.

8. Angie and Shane _____ near the school.

9. His teeth _____ white.

10. The elephants _____ outside.

***Check your answers with a partner and practice reading each sentence.
Pay close attention to where the digraphs are.

Supplemental
Component
p. 152-153

18.2 Complete the following sentences using ***is***, ***are***, or ***am***. Also, use the
correct preposition ***next to***, ***on***, ***in front of***, or ***near***.

Look at the picture and complete the sentences.

For example, "The woman is near the car."

1. The chicken _____ the car.

2. The cat _____ the car.

3. The shopping cart _____ the

car.

18.3 Practice with pronouns. Fill in the blanks using *is*, *are*, and *am*.

> *For example:*   *John* <u>*is*</u> *a student.*   *I* <u>*am*</u> *a student.*

1. It _____ an onion.

2. Sharon _____ a student.

3. Washington D.C. _____ a city.

4. He _____ a teacher.

5. We _____ friends.

6. It _____ ten o'clock.

7. I _____ hungry.

8. Robert and I _____ brothers.

9. Tom _____ 20 years old.

10. I _____ a lawyer.

11. She _____ my sister.

12. They _____ sick.

13. I _____ happy.

14. It _____ a newspaper.

15. He _____ from China.

16. We _____ soccer players.

17. Oscar and Adrian _____ cousins.

18. They _____ students.

19. I know her. She _____ in my class.

20. California _____ next to Oregon, Nevada and Arizona.

Supplemental Component p. 154

LET'S PRACTICE MORE

18.4 Remember there are 3 verbs "to be" — *is*, *are*, and *am*. Complete the sentences and practice reading them with a partner.

1. Heather _____ looking through her social media.
2. Charley and Sharon _____ in a virtual class.
3. Theo says, "I _____ leaving now."
4. Phillip _____ calling his brother now.
5. The doctors _____ discussing a new vaccine.
6. There _____ thirty-three doctors.
7. Chase _____ updating his profile.
8. Chuck and Thelma _____ chatting online.
9. Ming and I _____ signing the lease today.

18.5 Match the pronouns with the correct verb to be.

It

He

You

I

We

She

They

are

is

am

MORE PUNCTUATION PRACTICE: EXCLAMATION POINT!

18.6 When you are excited, use the exclamation point (!) to show you are saying something loudly or excitedly. Look at the example below.

It is cold outside!

You should notice two things about this sentence: 1) capitalization of the first word and 2) the end mark (exclamation point).

Look at the sentences below. They are all excited and said loudly. Rewrite them with the correct capitalization and exclamation point at the end. The first one is done for you.

1. i am happy to see you   <u>I am happy to see you!</u>

2. it is so hot outside   _____

3. please stop the bus   _____

4. slow down now   _____

5. watch out for the car   _____

6. wait for me   _____

Now, write three original sentences with excitement. Remember to capitalize and punctuate. For example, "Today is my birthday!"

1. _____

2. _____

3. _____

USING "A" AND "AN"

18.7 When do you use "a," and when do you use "an" before a noun? You use
"a" before a noun (or adjective) that begins with a consonant.
For example:

a dog   a building   a girl   a book

You use "an" before a noun that begins with a vowel. For example:
an elephant   an egg   an umbrella   an orange car

Look at the following nouns and place either "a" or "an" in front of the word.

1. _____ cat   5. _____ broom   9. _____ sandwich
2. _____ man   6. _____ apple   10. _____ octopus
3. _____ egg   7. _____ piano   11. _____ airplane
4. _____ day   8. _____ ice cream 12. _____ house

Now, complete the following sentences using either "a" or "an" in front of the noun or
adjective.

13. I am _____ good student.

14. She works in _____ supermarket.

15. Mr. John has _____ orange cat.

16. We live in _____ big house.

17. Sam rides _____ bus to class.

18. South Carolina is _____ state.

19. He is _____ Australian man.

20. Heather is _____ teacher.

21. Charley eats _____ sandwich.

MORE PRACTICE USING "A" AND "AN"

18.8 Look at the different food items and place either "a" or "an" in front of the word.

_____ olive

_____ hamburger

_____ sandwich

_____ egg

_____ ice cream cone

_____ tomato

_____ apple

_____ orange

_____ watermelon

_____ strawberry

_____ lemon

_____ carrot

_____ banana

_____ onion

_____ eggplant

_____ pizza

_____ hot dog

_____ bag of sugar

_____ cup of coffee

_____ American flag

_____ A.I. Picture

_____ pineapple

_____ old car

_____ loaf of bread

_____ eagle

_____ avocado

"EXCUSE ME, DO YOU KNOW THE TIME?"

TELLING TIME

 (Play Track 24)

Supplemental Component p. 155

19. Look at the time on the clocks. Listen and repeat.

12:00 PM

It's twelve o'clock.
It's noon.

9:00

It's nine o'clock.

3:15

It's three fifteen.
It's a quarter after three.

7:30

It's seven thirty.
It's half past seven.

1:45

It's one forty-five.
It's a quarter to two.

12:00 AM

It's midnight.
It's twelve in the morning.

ADDITIONAL PRACTICE

Use the QR code to practice pronunciation
improve your skills.

45

LEARNING THE TIMES OF DAY

 (Play Track 25)

19.1 Listen and repeat the times of day.

A.M.   <u>*in the morning*</u> *(12:00AM-11:59AM)*
7:00 AM - It's seven in the morning.
8:15 AM - It's eight fifteen in the morning.
10:30 AM - It's ten thirty in the morning.
11:45 AM - It's eleven forty-five in the morning.

P.M.   <u>*in the afternoon*</u> *(12:01PM-5:00PM)*
12:30 PM - It's twelve thirty in the afternoon.
3:45 PM - It's three forty-five in the afternoon.
4:00 PM - It's four o'clock in the afternoon.

P.M.   <u>*in the evening*</u> *(5:00PM-9:00PM)*
6:15 PM - It's a quarter after six in the evening.
7:10 PM - It's seven ten in the evening.
8:37 PM - It's eight thirty-seven in the evening.

P.M.   <u>*at night*</u> *(9:00PM-11:59PM)*
9:30 PM - It's nine thirty at night.
10:15 PM - It's ten fifteen at night.
11:45 PM - It's a quarter to midnight.

Look at the times. What time of day are they? Write "in the morning," "in the afternoon," or "in the evening" on the lines.

1. 5:30PM _____

2. 12:00PM _____

3. 8:20AM _____

4. 10:10PM _____

5. 6:50AM _____

6. 8:45PM _____

7. 11:00PM _____

8. 12:00AM _____

9. 3:12PM _____

10. 12:35PM _____

Supplemental Component p. 156

19.2 Remember, 15 minutes after an hour is often referred to as "a quarter after—."
15 minutes until the next hour is often referred to "a quarter to—."
For example, 5:15 would be "a quarter after 5," and 5:45 would be "a quarter to 6." Now, you try some.

1. 1:15 _____

2. 4:15 _____

3. 12:15 _____

4. 10:45 _____

5. 3:45 _____

6. 11:45 _____

7. 7:45 _____

8. 9:15 _____

CONVERSATION PRACTICE

 (Play Track 26)

19.3 Practice the short conversation with a partner.

Student 1: Excuse me. What time is it?
Student 2: <u>It's three o'clock.</u>
Student 1: Thank you.
Student 2: You're welcome.

Practice the conversation above and change the time using the times below. There may be more than one way to express the time.

(1) 12:00 AM	(4) 9:35 PM	(7) 11:25 AM
(2) 6:15 PM	(5) 10:11 AM	(8) 11:25 PM
(3) 8:15 AM	(6) 4:45 PM	(9) 12:00 PM

PRACTICE TIME USING "O"

 (Play Track 27)

19.4 When the time falls between :01 and :09, the proper way to say the time is by using "O" before the number. For example, for this time (12:01), you would say "twelve o' one." Look at the times below and repeat.

1. **3:03**　2. **8:01**　3. **7:07**　4. **6:06**

5. **12:09**　6. **5:07**　7. **4:08**　8. **1:05**

CONVERSATION PRACTICE

 (Play Track 28)

19.5 Practice the following short conversations with a partner.

1

A: Excuse me, can you tell me what time it is?

B: Yes. It's 12:05.

A: Thank you very much.

B: You're welcome.

2

A: Hi. Do you happen to know the time?

B: Sure. It's 7:09.

A: I appreciate it. Thank you.

 (Play Track 29)

19.6 Practice the short conversation with a partner. *Use "Sir" if your parter in male and "Ma'am" if your partner is female. Also, change the underlined times with 1-13.*

Student 1: Excuse me, "*Sir*." Do you know the time?
Student 2: Yes, it's <u>nine o' two</u>.
Student 1: <u>Nine o' two</u>? Wow. It's late. Thank you very much.
Student 2: No problem.

(1) 3:03 PM
(2) 1:12 PM
(3) 3:57 PM
(4) 10:12 AM
(5) 6:36 PM
(6) 6:01 AM
(7) 3:14 AM
(8) 7:59 PM
(9) 11:11 PM

(10)

(11)

(12)

(13)

ELAPSED TIME TABLE PRACTICE

19.7 Complete the time table. How much time has passed? The first one is done for you.

Start Time	End Time	Hours and Minutes
4:30 PM	5:41 PM	1 hour & 11 minutes
5:30 AM	7:00 AM	
6:30 PM	10:45 PM	
9:30 AM	10:44 AM	
2:00 PM		4 hours & 15 minutes
12:00 PM	4:25 PM	
	9:54 PM	3 hours & 39 minutes
11:30 PM		4 hours & 57 minutes
2:15 AM		2 hours & 12 minutes
6:30 PM	11:11 PM	
9:40 AM	7:10 PM	

THE VERB "TO BE" AND THE SIMPLE PRESENT TENSE

Supplemental Component p. 157

20. Study the following guide of Yes/No questions and complete the activities.

Questions				Answers						
Is	he she it				he she it	is.			he she it	isn't.
Are	you we they	on time?	Yes,		you we they	are.	No,		you we they	aren't.
Am	I				I	am.			I'm	not.

Combining *is*, *are*, and *am* with *not* is called *contracting*, using an apostrophe ('). For example:			
I + am = I'm	I + am + not = I'm not	you + are = you're	you + are + not = you aren't
he + is = he's	he + is + not = he isn't	we + are = we're	we + are + not = we aren't
she + is = she's	she + is + not = she isn't	they + are = they're	they + are + not = they aren't
it + is = it's	it + is + not = it isn't		

Use contractions for the following sentences. For example:

He is not here.   *He isn't here.*   (You can also write: *He's not here.*)

1. She is not late.   _____

2. It is not noon.   _____

3. We are not at home.   _____

4. You are in New York.   _____

5. No, he is not here.   _____

Answer the following questions. (Make them true about you. Use the guide.)

1. Is your teacher from Florida?   _____

2. Are you from El Salvador?   _____

3. Is it 5:00 PM now?   _____

4. Are your classmates from China?   _____

5. Is your class in the morning?   _____

20.1 Sentence scramble. The following sentences are not in the correct order. Rewrite the sentences in the correct order.

For example: are not / They / here.
<u>They are not here.</u> *OR* <u>They aren't here.</u>

1. is not / my / mother. / She

_____

2. work. / at / Yes, he is

_____

3. near / the ocean. / are not / Sam and I

_____

4. is not with / Thelma / the / doctors.

_____

5. are not / teachers. / Charley and Sharon

_____

6. home. / No, / Eva / is not

_____

Match the questions in column 1 with the correct answers in column 2.

1. _____ Is she late to class?   a. No, they aren't.

2. _____ Are they at work?   b. Yes, I am.

3. _____ Is John reading his book?   c. No, she isn't.

4. _____ Is it 7:00 PM now?   d. Yes, he is.

5. _____ Are you the teacher?   e. Yes, it is.

20.2 Listen, repeat and answer the following questions. Practice with a partner and make your responses true.

 (Play Track 30)

For example: A: Is it 5:00 PM?   A: Are they students?
                     B: _No, it isn't._   B: _Yes, they are._

1. Is your brother in class? _____

2. Is it hot outside? _____

3. Is it six in the evening? _____

4. Is today your birthday? _____

5. Is today Monday? _____

6. Are you from Africa? _____

20.3 Rewrite the following statements as questions.

For example:

    Chuck is home. ⟶ **_Is Chuck home?_**
    They are in school. ⟶ **_Are they in school?_**

~Don't forget the question mark at the end (?).

1. She is a student.   _____

2. I am in class.   _____

3. We are family.   _____

4. It is a quarter to six.   _____

5. You are from Cuba.   _____

6. He is on time.   _____

MORE PUNCTUATION PRACTICE: QUESTION MARK

20.4 Questions always end with a question mark (?). Look at the example below.

What is your name?

You should notice two things about this question. *Capitalization* of the first word and the end mark (question mark).

Look at the lines below. They are all questions. Rewrite them with the correct capitalization and question mark at the end. The first one is done for you.

1. is mary from canada   _____Is Mary from Canada?_____

2. what is your name   _____

3. are you sam   _____

4. where is the teacher   _____

5. who is from china   _____

6. when is your birthday   _____

Now, write three questions about your community. Remember to capitalize and punctuate. For example, "Where is the supermarket?"

1. _____

2. _____

3. _____

UNIT 2: COMPREHENSION CHECK

 (Play Track 31)

21. Listen to the conversations and answer the questions.

1. What time is it? A) 10:00   B) 1:00   C) 1:10

2. What time is his lunch break? A) 12:00 PM   B) 12:00 AM   C) 2:00 PM

3. When will he call? A) 3:25   B) 3:15   C) 3:45

4. What time does the man wake up? A) 5:00 PM   B) 5:05 AM   C) 5:00 AM

5. What time does the man get home from work? A) 7:30 AM   B) 7:30 PM   C) 7:00 PM

6. What time does he leave for school? A) 6:00   B) 5:45   C) 6:15

7. What time does the movie start? A) 7:00   B) 6:30   C) 7:30

8. What time does the store close? A) 9:00 AM   B) 9:00 PM   C) 8:00 PM

9. What time does the restaurant open? A) 5:00 AM   B) 5:00 PM   C) 12:00 PM

10. What time is it? A) 7:10   B) 10:07   B) 6:50

Look at the times below. Write the time of day for each. Use your notes.

For example: **8:15 AM**   *__in the morning__*

1. 9:30 PM   _____

2. 11:05 AM   _____

3. 6:27 PM   _____

4. 3:49 PM   _____

5. 12:00 AM   _____

6. 1:30 PM   _____

7. 7:00 PM   _____

8. 2:45 AM   _____

9. 12:00 PM   _____

10. 11:40 PM   _____

$$\frac{}{20}$$

DAYS / MONTHS / SEASONS

 (Play Track 32)

22. Look at the words. Listen and repeat.

1. Days of the Week	2. Months of the Year	
Sunday	January	August
Monday	February	September
Tuesday	March	October
Wednesday	April	November
Thursday	May	December
Friday	June	
Saturday	July	

22.1 Answer the following questions.

1. What day comes *before* Tuesday? _____

2. What day comes *after* Thursday? _____

3. What month is *between* September and July? _____

4. What month is *after* December? _____

5. What day is *between* Saturday and Monday? _____

22.2 Listen to the questions and write your answers. (Play Track 33)

1. _____

2. _____

3. _____

4. _____

5. _____

6. _____

7. _____

8. _____

9. _____

THE 4 SEASONS OF THE YEAR

23. There are four distinct seasons and they are as follows:

Spring	(March * April * May)
Summer	(June * July * August)
Autumn (Fall)	(September * October * November)
Winter	(December * January * February)

Spring for most places means fresh flowers and the beginning of the harvest season. It starts to get warmer, birds make nests, and flowers come out everywhere.

Summer is the time of year when it gets hot, people go on vacation and beaches everywhere get crowded. Days get longer because the sun it out more. Many fruits and vegetables are available at the market in larger quantities during the summer.

Fall gets its name because in the northern states, the leaves on trees fall off during the autumn months. It starts to get colder and the days get shorter because the sun sets earlier. In the fall, people get excited because the holidays and the end of the year celebrations begin.

Winter time in the north is very cold and snow falls in many places. States like New York, Pennsylvania, Ohio, Montana, Indiana and other northern states experience snow in the winter months. Other states like Florida, Alabama, Texas, South Carolina and Mississippi do not experience very cold weather. Winter in southern states gets cold, but snow is **rare**. (*Rare* means something that happens very little.)

23.1 Look at the pictures. What season do you think it is? Circle the correct answer.

1. (A) Winter
    (B) Summer

2. (A) Spring
    (B) Fall

3. (A) Fall
    (B) Summer

4. (A) Winter
    (B) Summer

PREPOSITIONS OF TIME: AT, ON, IN, AND FROM...TO

24. Complete the sentences with the correct preposition of time.

At	On	In
We use _at_ for **times**	We use _on_ for **dates** and **days**	We use _in_ for long periods of time
For example: _at_ 6 o'clock,	_For example_: _on_ Friday, _on_ May 10,	_For example_: _in_ 2013, _in_ the winter,
_at_ noon, _at_ lunchtime	_on_ Christmas Day, _on_ birthdays	_in_ the afternoon, _in_ September

From....To
We use _from...to_ for **times with a beginning and an end**
For example: I work _from_ 6:00 AM _to_ 5:00 PM.   I work _from_ Monday _to_ Friday.

For example: It's 10:00 **at** night.   I was born **on** July 26, 1971.

We have class **in** the morning.   We work **from** 8AM **to** 5PM.

1. Her birthday is _____ October 10.

2. We moved here _____ 2020.

3. The football game starts _____ 8:00 PM.

4. Valentine's Day is _____ February 14.

5. We are in class _____ 5:00 PM _____ 9:00 PM.

6. I will visit my family _____ the summer.

7. My father was born _____ the 1970's.

8. I get up _____ 7:00 AM _____ the morning.

9. I need to meet with her _____ 1:00 PM.

10. When is the meeting? Is it _____ 4:00 PM?

11. She gave me a nice present _____ Christmas Day.

12. We move to Washington _____ November.

24.1 Write the prepositions of time on the lines.

1. _____Thursday afternoon

2. _____ midnight

3. _____ 2024

4. _____ October 16

5. _____ November

6. _____ noon

7. _____ 4:00

8. _____ the morning

9. _____ 1998

10. _____ New Year's Eve

Complete the sentences using the prepositions of time.

1. Tom works _____ the evening.

2. He was born _____ Christmas Day.

3. The football game starts _____ 8 o'clock.

4. We can move _____ two weeks.

5. My class is _____ 9 AM _____ 11 AM.

6. I graduated from college _____ 2010.

7. Maria's birthday is _____ January.

8. The store closes _____ 10 PM.

9. They start work _____ 5:00 AM.

10. We wear heavy coats _____ winter.

Write three sentences of your own using prepositions of time.

1. _____

2. _____

3. _____

PRACTICE THE CONVERSATION

 (Play Track 34)

25. Telling the dates. Listen and repeat. Practice with a partner. Change the <u>meeting</u>, <u>date</u>, <u>time</u> and <u>locations</u> for more practice.

Meeting	Date	Time	Location
Job interview	Thursday, March 28	2:30 PM	Thrift Supermarket
Church Band	Tuesday, April 9	6:45 PM	Archbishop Church
English Testing	Friday, April 12	9:15 AM	Washington School
Work Training	Saturday , April 13	12:00 PM	Chuck Market
Soccer Practice	Monday, April 22	4:00 PM	Ring Field
Parent Night	Wednesday, May 8	5:00 PM	Chicago Academy

Pat: When do you meet for your <u>job interview</u>?

Sam: On <u>Thursday, March 28</u>.

Pat: What time?

Sam: At <u>2:30 in the afternoon</u>.

Pat: Where is your meeting?

Sam: At <u>Thrift Supermarket</u>.

26. Listen and repeat the conversation. Then, students can change the <u>underlined responses</u> with true information about themselves and practice with a partner.

 (Play Track 35)

Student A: Hi. What days do you study English?

Student B: I study English on <u>Tuesdays and Thursdays in the evenings</u>.

Student A: What times do you study English?

Student B: I study from <u>5:00 PM</u> to <u>9:00 PM</u>.

Student A: Wow. What time do you go to sleep?

Student B: I go to sleep at <u>11:00 PM</u>.

 (Play Tracks 36)

Thirteen.

Thirty.

26.1 Listen to the short conversations and match the questions with the correct responses.

Conversation #1

1. What time is the meeting? _____
2. When is the meeting? _____
3. Is the meeting time good for her? _____

a) on November 30   e) no
b) on November 13   f) yes
c) in 3 in the afternoon
d) at 3 in the afternoon

Conversation #2

4. What year was he born in? _____
5. When in his birthday? _____
6. What day is his birthday this year? _____

a) in 1917   e) on July 26
b) in 1971   f) at July 26
c) in a Saturday
d) on a Saturday

27. UNIT 2 ASSESSMENT

 (Play Track 37)

Part 1:

Look at the pictures and listen to the recording. Circle the correct answer: A, B, or C.

1.

A

B

C

2.

A

B

C

Part 2:

Listen and Write: Listen to the conversations and answer the questions.

1. What time is it? _____

2. What time does he go to work? _____

3. What day is the party? _____

4. When is the show? _____

5. What time does his mother arrive? _____

Part 3:

Look at the times below and match the time in column A with the correct time of day in column B.

Column A	Column B
1. _____10:00 AM	A. Noon
2. _____11:00 AM	B. Eleven in the morning
3. _____3:30 PM	C. Nine o' two at night
4. _____7:15 PM	D. Twenty after twelve in the morning
5. _____12:00 PM	E. Three thirty in the afternoon
6. _____5:45 PM	F. A quarter to six in the evening
7. _____12:20 AM	G. Half past four in the afternoon
8. _____4:30 PM	H. Midnight
9. _____9:02 PM	I. Ten o'clock in the morning
10._____12:00 AM	J. Quarter after seven in the evening

UNIT 3

CALENDAR, DATES, OCCUPATIONS

In this section, we will cover:
– *Ordinal Numbers*
– *Calendar / Appointments*
– *Consonant Blends*
– *Occupations*
– *The Future Tense (will)*
– *The Digraphs KN and QU*

first ⟶ 1st

second ⟶ 2nd

third ⟶ 3rd

fourth ⟶ 4th

bl

br

cl

st

sp

fl

REVIEW LONG AND SHORT VOWELS

 (Play Track 38)

28. Practice the long and short vowels.

Say:	A	E	I	O	U
Long	ā	ē	ī	ō	ū
Short	ă	ĕ	ĭ	ŏ	ŭ

28.1 Introduction to the phonetic symbol / 3: /. (Play Track 39)

This is the sound in the word _Bird_.

Listen and repeat.   Bird   Word   Heard   Third   Dirt   Learn

These words use the / 3: / "er" sound. Listen and repeat the following words.

1. Girl

2. Early

3. Sir

4. Thirty

5. Burn

6. Water

7. Tower

8. Circle

9. Finger

10. Turtle

11. Feather

12. Shirt

13. Hammer

14. Exercise

15. Squirrel

16. River

17. Mermaid

18. Her

19. Faster

20. Spider

Supplemental Component p. 158

NEW VOCABULARY WORDS: ORDINAL NUMBERS

29. Look at the words. Listen and repeat. **(Play Track 40)**

1. First - 1st
2. Second - 2nd
3. Third - 3rd
4. Fourth - 4th
5. Fifth - 5th
6. Sixth - 6th
7. Seventh - 7th
8. Eighth - 8th
9. Ninth - 9th
10. Tenth - 10th
11. Eleventh - 11th
12. Twelfth - 12th

13. Thirteenth - 13th
14. Fourteenth - 14th
15. Fifteenth - 15th
16. Sixteenth - 16th
17. Seventeenth - 17th
18. Eighteenth - 18th
19. Nineteenth - 19th
20. Twentieth - 20th
21. Twenty-first - 21st
22. Twenty-second - 22nd
23. Twenty-third - 23rd
24. Twenty-fourth - 24th

25. Twenty-fifth - 25th
26. Twenty-sixth - 26th
27. Twenty-seventh - 27th
28. Twenty-eighth - 28th
29. Twenty-ninth - 29th
30. Thirtieth - 30th
31. Thirty-first - 31st

Supplemental
Component
p. 159-160

29.1 Match the ordinal numbers. Then, practice saying each one.

_____ 1. Ninth   a.   1st

_____ 2. Nineteenth   b.   7th

_____ 3. Twentieth   c.   9th

_____ 4. Seventh   d.   23rd

_____ 5. Twenty-eighth   e.   10th

_____ 6. Thirtieth   f.   19th

_____ 7. First   g.   30th

_____ 8. Tenth   h.   20th

_____ 9. Twenty-third   i.   28th

THE CALENDAR  (Play Track 41)

30. When you say dates, the number is said as an ordinal number. For example, "The second of May" or "May second."

Practice saying the dates. Listen and repeat.

July 4	*December 25*	*November 21*
October 31	*May 5*	*January 3*
February 14	*April 1*	*September 16*

30.1 Conversation with a partner. Listen, repeat, then practice.

 (Play Track 42)

Pat: Sam, when is your birthday?

Sam: My birthday is on Thursday.

Pat: What's the date on Thursday?

Sam: Thursday is August 13th.

Pat: August 13th?

Sam: Yes. I was born on August 13th, 1990.

Pat: I was also born in 1990.

Sam: When is your birthday, Pat?

Pat: My birthday is in December.

Sam: When in December?

Pat: I was born on December 2nd.

Sam: That means I am older than you.

Pat: Yes, you are almost four months older than me.

Supplemental Component: p.161

THE 30 DAY SONG

 (Play Track 43)

30.2 There are 365 days a year.

Do you know how many days are in each month?
Well, here's a fun way to remember. Sing along.

> 30 days has September
>
> April, June and November
>
> The rest has 31 days, you see?
>
> Except February

NEW VOCABULARY WORDS

 (Play Track 44)

30.3 Important dates on the calendar. Listen and repeat.

1. doctor's appointment
2. job interview
3. dentist appointment
4. rent due
5. mother visits

6. light bill due
7. New Year's Day
8. holiday
9. birthday party
10. concert

67

A MONTHLY SCHEDULE

Look at the calendar below to do the activities and answer the questions related to Eva's schedule in the month of January in Sections 31-32.

Eva's Schedule for **January**

Sun	Mon	Tue	Wed	Thu	Fri	Sat
		1 holiday *New Year's Day*	**2**	**3**	**4**	**5** rent due
6	**7** job interview 1:00 PM	**8**	**9**	**10**	**11**	**12**
13 birthday party 5:00 PM	**14**	**15**	**16**	**17** doctor's appointment 12:30 PM	**18**	**19** concert 9:00 PM
20	**21**	**22**	**23** light bill due	**24**	**25** mother visits 6:00 PM	**26**
27	**28**	**29** dentist appointment 3:15 PM	**30**	**31**		

LISTENING PRACTICE

 (Play Track 45)

31. Listen to the recordings about Eva and look at the calendar. Circle true or false.

1.   true   false

2.   true   false

3.   true   false

4.   true   false

5.   true   false

 (Play Track 46)

32. Listen to the conversations and repeat. Work with a partner and reference the information from Eva's calendar.

1

Sam: Hi, Eva. I was wondering, would you have lunch with me on Thursday?

Eva: Lunch on Thursday, the 17th?

Sam: Yes, the 17th.

Eva: Sorry, Sam. I have a doctor's appointment at that time.

Sam: That's okay. Some other time, then?

Eva: Sure!

69

 (Play Track 47)

2

Sam: Hello, Eva. I was wondering, would you
    have dinner with me on Friday?
Eva: Dinner on Friday, the 25th?
Sam: Yes, the 25th.
Eva: Sorry, Sam. My mother is visiting at that time.
Sam: That's okay. Some other time, then?
Eva: Yes, that would be nice.

 (Play Track 48)

3

Sam: How are you, Eva? I was wondering, would you have
    lunch with me on Monday?
Eva: Lunch on Monday, the 7th?
Sam: Yes, the 7th.
Eva: Sorry, Sam. I have a job interview at that time.
Sam: That's okay. Some other time, then?
Eva: Ok!

 (Play Track 49)

4

Sam: What's up, Eva? I was wondering, would you have dinner
    with me on Sunday?
Eva: Dinner on Sunday, the 13th?
Sam: Yes, the 13th.
Eva: Sorry, Sam. It's my birthday on Sunday and I am having
    a party at that time.
Sam: That's okay. Some other time, then?
Eva: Well, why don't you come to my party?
Sam: Really? I can come to your party?
Eva: Yes. It will be a lot of fun.
Sam: Great! See you Sunday!

32.1 Make your own schedule. Look at the blank calendar. Label the calendar for the following month and write the dates from the first to the last day of the month. For example, if it is November now, make the calendar for December from the 1st to the 31st. Then, mark your scheduled appointments for the month. Use the vocabulary words in Section 30 and Eva's calendar as a guide.

Month

Sun	Mon	Tue	Wed	Thu	Fri	Sat

32.2 After completing your own calendar and schedule, answer the following questions.

1. What day of the week is the 9th? _____

2. How many Fridays are there in the month? _____

3. What is your first appointment of the month? _____

4. What is your last appointment of the month? _____

71

LISTENING PRACTICE

 (Play Track 50)

32.3 Listen to the phone conversations. Then, answer the questions with the correct information.

Conversation #1: Making an appointment

1. What doctor does the man want to see?   A) Dr. Smith   B) Dr. Quiñonez   C) Dr. Patel
2. What is the date of the appointment? _____
3. What time is the appointment? _____

Conversation #2: Canceling an appointment

1. Who is the appointment with? A) Dr. Smith   B) Dr. Quiñonez   C) Dr. Patel
2. Does the man want to reschedule the appointment? _____
3. What was the date of the appointment? _____

32.4 Look at the card below. It has information about Sam's appointment. Answer questions 1-5 using the information on the card.

_____
Sam Salvador
My appointment is on

☐ Mon   ☒ Tue   ☐ Wed   ☐ Thu   ☐ Fri

Date___January 8th___ At ___10___ (AM) PM

Dr. Patel
444 Main Street, Suite A
Baltimore, MD 21223
(410) 555-4567

If you are unable to keep your appointment, please give us 24 hour notice.

1. When is Sam's appointment?

_____

2. What time is his appointment?

_____

3. Who is Sam's doctor?

_____

4. What is the address?

_____

5. What is the phone number?

_____

LISTENING CHALLENGE  (Play Track 51)

32.5 Listen to the conversation between Paula and her doctor. Then, answer the questions.

Questions

1. What is wrong with Paula? A) she feels good   B) she feels sick   C) she needs work

2. When did she start feeling sick? A) 1 day ago B) 2 days ago   C) three days ago

3. How does the doctor examine her? A) checks her lungs and heart B) checks her eyes

C) checks her mouth

4. What does the doctor say? A) "you need to go to the hospital" B) "everything sounds

Ok"   C) "everything sounds fine"

5. What does the doctor recommend? A) drink lots of water and rest   B) go to work

C) eat lots of food

6. What does Paula ask for? A) permission to return to work   B) an excuse from work

C) permission to sleep in the doctor's office

PHONIC POINTS

Consonant Blends

These socks have stripes.

This is a blue crab.

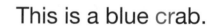

This square is red.

CONSONANT BLENDS

 (Play Track 52)

33. Consonant blends are two or three different consonant letters put together in a word and each letter sound is heard when the word is pronounced. For example, in the word "splash," you hear the "s," the "p," and the "l" individually. Listen and repeat the following sets of words that have consonant blends.

1. (SL)	slice	sleep	12. (SP)	spend	clasp
2. (FL)	flower	Florida	13. (ST)	fast	stay
3. (CL)	clean	clock	14. (SW)	swing	sweep
4. (GL)	glass	glad	15. (TW)	twist	twelve
5. (FR)	fry	free	16. (SPL)	split	splash
6. (BR)	broom	brain	17. (SCR)	scrape	scratch
7. (CR)	crab	cry	18. (SPR)	spread	sprinkle
8. (DR)	drag	drain	19. (SQU)	square	squeeze
9. (TR)	trash	travel	20. (STR)	street	straw
10. (BL)	blanket	blue	21. (THR)	three	throw
11. (PR)	pray	price	22. (SHR)	shred	shrimp

The following three sets of words have consonant blends that sound like /sk/.

1. (SC)	scoop	screen	3. (SCH)	school	schedule
2. (SK)	task	skim			

Practice these words and define what they mean in your first language. This will help you when you want use them in conversations.

CONVERSATION PRACTICE

 (Play Track 53)

33.1 Listen to the following short conversation and repeat. Then, practice with a partner.

Student A: Excuse me. Where is the Florida school?

Student B: It's on twelfth street.

Student A: Do I have to travel very far?

Student B: It's just about three blocks away. If you walk fast, you can get there

in a few minutes.

Student A: Thank you very much.

Student B: Oh, you are very welcome.

| sc | cr | tw | sl | br | cl | shr | str | tr |

33.2 Fill in the blanks with the correct beginning consonant blends.

_____imp

_____ash

_____ab

_____ock

_____ain

_____eep

_____oop

_____aw

_____elve

CROSSWORD PUZZLE

33.3 Complete the crossword puzzle using two and three letter consonant blends.

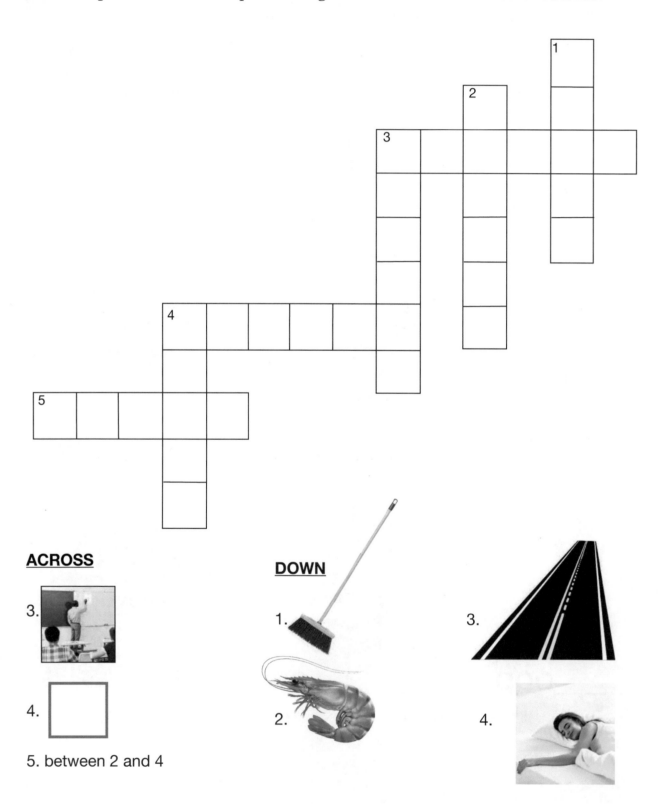

ACROSS

3.

4.

5. between 2 and 4

DOWN

1.

2.

3.

4.

UNIT 3: COMPREHENSION CHECK

 (Play Track 54)

34. Listen to the conversations and answer to the questions. You will hear each conversation two times.

1. What time does he work on Saturday?

2. When is his rent due?

3. When will Mary be here?

4. When will Manuel clean the car?

5. Where will Sam be after lunch?

6. When is her dentist appointment?

7. Where will Eva be on the 9th?

8. What is Eva looking for?

9. What is the man looking for?

10. When does Kevin play football?

11. What does she like to do on her free time?

12. What is the man listening to?

13. Will Steve be at the class party tomorrow?

14. Is Sam working this weekend?

15. Is it going to rain tomorrow?

	Mark answers in bubbles.	
	A B C	A B C
	1 ○○○	11 ○○○
	2 ○○○	12 ○○○
	3 ○○○	13 ○○
	4 ○○○	14 ○○
	5 ○○○	15 ○○
	6 ○○○	
	7 ○○○	
	8 ○○○	
	9 ○○○	
	10 ○○○	

HOW DO YOU LOOK FOR A JOB?

The job market changes with the demands of the day. With the environment in mind, new categories of jobs have entered the job market. Workers with skills in the technology field have more opportunities to find work.

OCCUPATIONS (WORK)

 (Play Track 55)

35. There are many types of jobs. Some people work outside; some inside. Some people work at home or "remotely." These are considered indoor jobs. Here are some different kinds of occupations around the city. Which do you think are done indoors (or "inside) and which are done outside? Some may be both.
Listen and repeat.

1. Plumber

2. Mover

3. Painter

4. Cashier

5. Waiter

6. Clinical Nurse

7. Solar Panel Installer

8. Park Ranger

9. Researcher

INDOOR/OUTDOOR JOBS AND IDENTIFYING SKILLS

 (Play Track 56)

35.1 Practice reading about each job. Point to the consonant blends, digraphs, and vowels. Listen and repeat.

Jobs with **Consonant Blends**:

1. Plexico is a plumber. He fixes pipes.
2. Clory is a clinical nurse. She helps sick people.
3. Sal is a solar panel installer. He installs solar panels on houses.

Jobs with **Digraphs**:

4. Shirley is a cashier. She works in a supermarket.
5. Charley is a childcare worker. She works with little children.
6. Raul is a researcher. He studies the environment.

Jobs with **Long / a /**:

7. Peter is a painter. He paints houses six days a week.
8. Wayne is a waiter. He works in a restaurant.
9. Betty is a baker. She bakes cookies, cakes and breads every day.

Plumber	Clinical Nurse	Solar Panel Installer
Cashier	Childcare Worker	Researcher
Painter	Waiter	Baker

35.2 Look at the pictures and match them with the name of their occupation.
For example:

• Mechanic

• Construction Worker

• Cook/Chef

• Fire Fighter

• Truck Driver

35.3 Match the description with its occupation. For example:

_x_ He fixes pipes. ←——————————————→ x. plumber

1. ____ She bakes cakes.

2. ____ He drives a truck.

3. ____ She helps sick people.

4. ____ He puts out fires.

5. ____ She comes when you call 911.

6. ____ He paints houses.

7. ____ He installs solar panels.

8. ____ He moves furniture.

9. ____ She serves food.

a. Police officer

b. Solar panel installer

c. Fire fighter

d. Baker

e. Waiter

f. Truck driver

g. Nurse

h. Painter

i. Mover

35.4 Read the following paragraph and answer the questions.

Tony is a security guard. He works at a hotel. His friend Tom works at the same hotel. Tom is the maintenance worker. Tom's wife, Nana, works at the supermarket across from the hotel. Nancy is a cashier. Tony's wife, Glenda, works with Nancy. Glenda is the store manager. She works in the evenings.

1. What is Tom's occupation? _____

2. What is Glenda's occupation? _____

3. What is Tony's occupation? _____

4. What is Nancy's occupation? _____

5. When does Glenda work? _____

WHAT KIND OF JOB DO YOU DREAM OF?

35.5 Talk with your classmates about the types of jobs that interest you. Why are these jobs interesting and how do they impact others (or the environment)?

After your discussion, answer the following questions.

1. What is one job that is interesting to you? _____

2. Why is this job interesting to you? _____

3. How does this job impact others? _____

_____

4. What level of education does someone need for this kind of job? _____

_____

SHOULD AND SHOULDN'T

should not = shouldn't

35.6 *When do you use "should" and when do you use "shouldn't?"*

Question: Is it good to text and drive?

We use should and shouldn't to give advice on what we think is right or wrong. We also use them to guide others when making important decisions. Here are some example:

- You shouldn't use your phone when driving a car.

- You should eat healthy foods and exercise regularly.

- You shouldn't throw trash in the oceans.

- You should finish school and graduate.

- You shouldn't spend more money than you can afford.

- You should help others when you can.

Can you think of some things you "should" or "shouldn't" do? Write two below.

_____

_____

SEARCHING FOR A JOB

Discussion

36. If you need a job, where do you look?

ONLINE

Job posting online can be found on many websites. Sometimes just typing "jobs" in the search bar of any search engine will result in several listings on various websites and platforms.

SIGNS

Sometimes businesses will put signs on the front window to let people know they are hiring.

JOB FAIRS

Job fairs are events where employers give information to potential employees. Job fairs are excellent opportunities to connect with more than one employer at a time in one location.

What are some other places you can search for a job?

36.1 Look at the job advertisement below and answer the questions.

1. Where is the new location? A) downtown   B) uptown   C) across town

2. What do the jobs pay? A) $10 an hour   B) $12-$14 an hour   C) $17-21$ an hour

3. What is the address? _____

4. What time should you apply? _____

5. List the things you need to qualify for this job. _____

_____

_____

_____

THE APPLICATION PROCESS

36.2 Read the paragraph about Eva.

There is a "Help Wanted" sign on the front window of the *Taco Rey* restaurant. Eva asks to talk to the manager. The manager says they need a waiter. He asks her to "fill out" an application.

Look at Eva's application and answer the questions.

Employment Application Form	Application Date
General Information	3/3/2025

Last name	First Name	Initial	Social Security No.
Torres	Eva	M.	000-55-1234

Address	Home Telephone
636 Baltimore Road	410-555-0123

City, State, Zip Code	Salary Desired
Baltimore, MD 21231	$18 / Hour

Position Applying For	Hours Available	Date Available
Waiter	4PM - Midnight	3/3/2025

Are you at least 18 years of age? [X] Yes ☐ No

Education Information

High School	Address	Studies	Graduated?
Patterson Academy	180 Eastern Ave.	Business	Yes

College	Address	Studies	Graduated?
County College	903 Rossville Drive	Hospitality	No

Employment History

Date of most recent employer: from 2/1/24 to 12/9/2024

Name of employer	Position held	Salary
Rosita's Restaurant	Waiter	$15/hour

Job duties (describe your responsibilities)

Customer orders and serve food

Reason for leaving

Medical reasons

Other information

Volunteer activities

I volunteer at the English learning center teaching immigrants.

Hobbies, interests, etc.

I play piano for fun at parties.

I hearty acknowledge the information above is true.

Eva Marie Torres   3/3/25

Signature   Date

---

1. What is Eva's address? _____

2. What is Eva's most recent employer? _____

3. When did she work there? _____

4. Why did Eva leave her last job? _____

5. What salary does Eva desire? _____

36.3 Fill out this application with your information for practice. Fill in all the details.

Complete this application for a job at Taco Rey. Pretend you are applying for a position at the restaurant. For example, you may want to be a cook, or a cashier, or waiter. Use Eva's application as a guide to complete your own application. Remember, this is just practice. Ask your teacher for help.

Employment Application	Application Date

General Information

_____

Last name	First Name	Initial	Social Security No.

Address		Home Telephone	

City, State, Zip Code		Salary Desired	

Position Applying For	Hours Available	Date Available

Are you at least 18 years of age? ☐ Yes ☐ No

Education Information

High School	Address	Studies	Graduated?

College	Address	Studies	Graduated?

36.3
Continued

Complete as many details as you can. Don't forget to sign and date the bottom of the application.

Employment History

Date of most recent Employer: From _____ to _____

Name of Employer   Position Held   Salary

_____

Job Duties (Describe your responsibilities.)

_____

Reason for leaving

_____

Other Information

Volunteer activities

_____

Hobbies, interests, etc.

_____

I hereby acknowledge the information above is true.

_____

Signature   Date

FUTURE TENSE USING "WILL"

Supplemental
Component
p. 162-164

37. Using "will" signifies an action that has not happened yet. Use the chart as a guide to help you complete the sentences.

Affirmative Statements				Negative Statements			
I		work		I		work	
You		travel		You		travel	
He		stay		He		stay	
She	*will*	play	*tonight*.	She	*will not*	play	*tomorrow*.
It		fly		It	*won't*	fly	
We		leave		We		leave	
They		go		They		go	

Contractions. In Section 20, we combined the pronouns *is*, *am* and *are* using an apostrophe. For the future tense, combine pronouns with "will" also using an apostrophe. For example:

I + will = I'll	will + not = won't	you + will = you'll	he + will = he'll
she + will = she'll	it + will = it'll	we + will = we'll	they + will = they'll

Complete the sentences using contractions in the future tense.

1. (I will) _____ go to a job interview tomorrow.

2. (They will) _____ leave work at 5:00 PM.

3. (She will) _____ help you in five minutes.

4. (It will) _____ snow tonight.

5. (We will) _____ spend more time together.

6. (will not) Mary says she _____ work next week.

CONVERSATION PRACTICE: TURN AND TALK

 **(Play Track 57)**

37.1 Listen to the following conversation and repeat. Then, practice with a partner.

A: When I travel to Florida, I spend a lot of time at the beach. It's great to splash in the warm waters.

B: I love Florida. I always eat lots of crabs and shrimp there. The prices aren't too expensive.

A: Florida is also famous for oranges. I squeeze them and make fresh juice.

B: Fresh orange juice is great, you're right. When will you travel there again?

A: I will spend three weeks in Miami in November.

B: Wow. You are lucky.

Answer the questions following the conversation.

1. Where will the woman be in November? _____

2. What does the man eat in Florida? _____

3. What does the woman squeeze to make fresh juice? _____

4. How long will the woman spend in Miami? _____

5. What does the woman do when she visits Florida? _____

_____

MORE PRACTICE WITH "WILL"

37.2 Rewrite the sentences in the future tense using "will" and also the simple present tense. If the verb in the simple present has an "-s," then it should not have it in the future tense. Look at the first two. They are already complete.

Simple Present Tense   Future Tense

Simple Present Tense	Future Tense
I work at 7:00 AM.	I will work at 7:00 AM.
She walks home.	She will walk home.
He eats pizza for lunch.	
They work tonight.	
Sam visits Eva on Tuesday.	
	Mary will sleep at 9:00 PM.
	The store will open at 10:30AM.
John sweeps the floor on Monday.	
	Adesh will turn 25 years old tomorrow.
Jorge and Sam ride the bus.	

Now write your own sentences. First, in the simple present tense, then future with will.

For example: I practice English.   I will practice English.

1. _____   _____
2. _____   _____
3. _____   _____

38. UNIT 3 LISTENING QUIZ

Part 1:  (Play Track 58)

Look at the pictures and listen to the recordings. Match the picture that best goes with the information and circle either the letter *A*, *B*, or *C*.

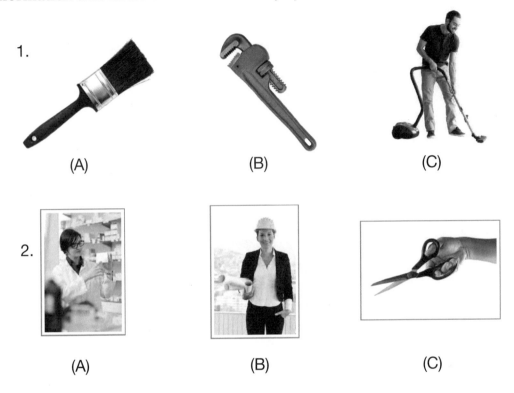

1.

(A)   (B)   (C)

2.

(A)   (B)   (C)

Part 2:

Listen to the conversations and answer the questions. Circle either A, B, or C.

1. What is the man's occupation? A) waiter   B) firefighter   C) truck driver

2. When is the man's interview? A) 2:30   B) 12:30   C) 10:30

3. How many years experience does the man have? A) six   B) seven   C) sixteen

4. When can the man start working? A) January 4th   B) January 16th   C) January 14th

5. What will Manuel be doing on Saturday? A) working   B) at a party   C) at a job interview

6. What job will the man apply for? A) cook   B) Rosita's Restaurant   C) Manuel

THE DIGRAPHS QU AND KN

 (Play Track 59)

39. Let's begin with practicing the pronunciation of the digraphs QU and KN.

Digraph	Sounds Like	Example
QU	/ k w /	*Question*
KN	/ n /	*Know*

Look at the pictures and practice saying the words.

1. Quarter

2. Squid

3. Aqua

4. Queen

5. Knife

6. Knee

7. Knob

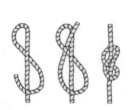

8. Knots

PRACTICE PRONUNCIATION  (Play Track 60)

39.1 Point to the words that have digraphs and practice repeating them.

That	Love	Sing	Known
Shower	Tooth	Black	Dress
Shrimp	Quart	Cry	Quality

39.2 Look at the words below. They are words with the digraphs QU and KN. Listen and repeat.

 (Play Track 61)

KN	QU
1. Knock	11. Quick
2. Kneel	12. Quart
3. Knuckle	13. Quality
4. Unknown	14. Require
5. Knowledge	15. Quiet
6. Knot	16. Equipment
7. Knockdown	17. Quit
8. Knee	18. Quota
9. Knob	19. Qualify
10. Knight	20. Quiz

Supplemental Component p. 165

PRACTICE READING SENTENCES  (Play Track 62)

39.3 Practice the sentences. Listen and repeat.

1. This equipment is for cleaning the floors.
2. The quality of my work is important.
3. I fell down and hurt my knee.
4. Knock on the door before you enter.
5. With your experience, you qualify for the job.
6. Mario wants to quit his job.
7. I will reach my quota of selling twenty cars today.
8. The rabbit is quick.
9. I will buy a quart of milk tonight.
10. Turn the knob and open the door.

39.4 Fill in the blanks with the correct digraphs.

kn qu

1. Shh. Be _____iet.

2. The chicken is ____ick.

3. The soldier ____eels.

4. It's warehouse e____ipment.

5. This is my ____uckle.

6. This car is high ____ality.

PRACTICE THE CONVERSATION

 (Play Track 63)

39.5 Listen to the following short conversation and repeat. Then, practice with a partner.

Mr. Quinn: Hi Tony. I have a question. I need you to work on Saturday. Will you be available?

Tony: Yes, Mr. Quinn, I will be available. What time do you need me?

Mr. Quinn: I need you to come in at four in the afternoon.

Tony: That's fine, Mr. Quinn. Will it be for eight hours?

Mr. Quinn: Yes, eight hours. Thank you, Tony.

Tony: It's quite alright.

Answer the following questions.

1. When does Mr. Quinn want Tony to work? _____

2. How many hours will Tony work? _____

3. What time will Tony finish his shift? _____

MORE CONVERSATION PRACTICE

 (Play Track 64)

39.6 Listen to the following conversation and repeat. Then, practice with a partner.

Ms. Knowles: I'm glad Mr. Quinn knows we will work all hours of the day.

Tom: Yes, and Mr. Quinn knows we all work hard.

Ms. Knowles: This is true. I think it's because we love our jobs.

Tom: Yes, I agree. Ms. Knowles, do you know where the new equipment is?

Ms. Knowles: New equipment? What new equipment?

Tom: We have three new vacuum cleaners.

Ms. Knowles: Oh, those? They are in the back of the equipment room.

USING "CAN" AND "CAN'T"

40. Using "can" and "can't" says whether are able to do something or not. Use the chart as a guide to help you comprehend how to use *can* and *can't* in sentences.

Affirmative Statements				Negative Statements			
You				You			
She				She			
He				He			
We	*can*	go	home.	We	*cannot*	go	home.
You		play	soccer.	You	*can't*	play	soccer.
They				They			
I				I			

40.1 Read the following story and complete the sentences using can or can't.

Jesus is a musician from Honduras. He can play many different instruments. He can play the guitar. He also plays the trumpet and the drums. He loves the piano, but he cannot play the piano. Jesus has a good voice and can sing. He says he will learn how to play the violin soon.

Supplemental
Component
p. 166

1. Jesus _____ play the guitar.

2. He _____ play the trumpet.

3. He loves the piano, but he _____ play it.

4. Jesus _____ play the drums.

5. He _____ play the violin.

6. Jesus _____ sing.

SENTENCE SCRAMBLE

40.2 The following sentences are not in the correct order.
Rewrite the sentences in the correct order. Change "cannot" to "can't."

For example: cannot / run / fast. / Yolanda
<u>Yolanda   can't   run   fast.</u>

1. sing. / cannot / Brian

_____

2. home. / go / We / cannot

_____

3. today. / The boys / play / can / soccer

_____

4. cannot / Thelma / call / home.

_____

5. cannot / teachers. / They / help / the

_____

6. leave work / Yes, Eva can / now.

_____

Match the questions in column 1 with the correct answers in column 2.

1. _____ Can she come now?   a. No, they can't.

2. _____ Can they use the table?   b. Yes, I can.

3. _____ Can John have this book?   c. No, he can't.

4. _____ Can we come at 7:00 PM?   d. Yes, she can.

5. _____ Can you call the teacher?   e. Yes, we can.

DEMONSTRATE UNDERSTANDING: CAN / CAN'T

40.3 Look at the examples below. Use *can* and *can't* to talk about abilities in the present tense.

> My name is Kashi and I love sports. I can play soccer and basketball. I can play volleyball too because we play this at my school. I can't play golf and I am not good at tennis. I can't speak Spanish or French, but I can speak English and German.

I. Read the statements. Circle if they are true or false.

1. She can play soccer.   TRUE   FALSE

2. She can't play volleyball.   TRUE   FALSE

3. She can play tennis.   TRUE   FALSE

4. She can play volleyball.   TRUE   FALSE

5. She can speak German.   TRUE   FALSE

6. She can't speak Spanish.   TRUE   FALSE

II. Complete the sentences by circling either CAN or CAN'T.

1. People can / can't breathe under water.

2. Elephants can / can't ride a bike.

3. Rabbits can / can't run fast.

4. Dogs can / can't fly.

5. People can / can't ride horses.

MORE READING PRACTICE

Meet Pat.

40.4 Read the story and answer the questions with complete sentences.

Pat is a new student from China. He wants to move to Los Angeles, California to be with his family. Right now, he lives in Chicago, Illinois. He likes to work on the computer and read the news. He wants to go to the university when he moves to California. He wants to study to be a medical doctor.

Write the answers to the questions in complete sentences on the lines.

For example: Where is Pat from? He is from China.

1. Where does Pat want to move? _____

2. What does Pat like to read? _____

3. Where does Pat live now? _____

4. What are three reasons Pat want to move to California?

_____

_____

_____

READING PRACTICE

Meet Sam.

40.5 Read the story and answer the questions.

This is Sam. He is from Fairfax, Virginia. He lives with his mother and father. He works in construction. It is hard work. Sam goes to school on Tuesdays and Thursdays after work. His teacher's name is Professor Johnson.

Answer "yes" or "no" to the following questions.

1. _____ Sam is from Washington, D.C.

2. _____ Sam lives with his mother and father.

3. _____ Sam works in construction.

Write the answers to the following questions.

4. When does Sam go to school? _____

5. Where is Sam from? _____

6. What is his teacher's name? _____

OCCUPATION TOOLS  (Play Track 65)

41. Identify tools used for various jobs.

| 1. Wrench | 2. Hammer | 3. Paint Brush | 4. Screw Driver | 5. Pliers | 6. Ratchet |

7. Lawn Mower

The man uses a lawn mower to cut the grass.

8. Shovel

The man uses a shovel to dig up dirt.

9. Saw

The man uses a saw to cut wood.

41.1 Answer the following questions with "Yes, you can," or "No, you can't."

1. Can you use a shovel to dig up dirt? _____

2. Can you use a wrench to cut wood? _____

3. Can you use a lawn mower to cut the grass? _____

4. Can you use pliers to paint the walls? _____

5. Can you use a hammer to fix your phone? _____

6. Can you use a screw driver to take out screws? _____

42. UNIT 3 ASSESSMENT  (Play Track 66)

Part 1:

Look at the pictures and listen. Circle the correct answer. Is the correct answer *A*, *B*, or *C*?

1.

A

B

C

2.

A

B

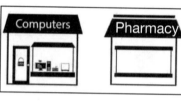
C

Part 2:

Listen to the conversations. Listen again and answer the questions. You will hear everything two times.

Drill #1

1. What time is it?

2. When is the man's appointment?

3. What day is today?

Drill #2

4. What is the man's occupation?

5. How many years experience is required?

6. What much milk does the man need?

Use this answer sheet.

Unit 3:

Listening Drills 1 and 2

Circle the best answer to the questions.
For example: A   B   (C)

1. A   B   C

2. A   B   C

3. A   B   C

4. A   B   C

5. A   B   C

6. A   B   C

UNIT 4

MONEY, CLOTHES, COLORS, HOLIDAYS AND SAFETY

In this section, we will cover:
– Diphthongs
– Money
– Identifying Clothes and Colors
– Foods
– Holidays
– Safety Signs

WHAT ARE DIPHTHONGS?

 (Play Track 67)

43. Diphthongs include the following pairs of letters: ***au, aw, ew, ow, oi, ou***, and ***oy***. There are actually two "ow" sounds. Practice the following sets of diphthongs. Listen and repeat.

1. C<u>ow</u>

2. B<u>oy</u>

3. H<u>ouse</u>

4. P<u>oi</u>son

5. S<u>aw</u>

6. J<u>ew</u>elry

7. S<u>au</u>ce

8. B<u>ow</u>

MORE PRONUNCIATION PRACTICE

 (Play Track 68)

43.1 Listen and repeat the following words with diphthongs.

ow	oy	ou	oi	ew
Owl	Joy	House	Join	Few
Clown	Toy	Mouth	Soil	Crew
Town	Royal	Pound	Boil	Chew
Flowers	Enjoy	Blouse	Coin	Screw

aw	au
Lawn	Autumn
Yawn	Auto
Hawk	Fault
Crawl	Audio

43.2 Complete the following sentences using words from the word bank. Then, practice reading the sentences with a partner.

> **house   boil   clown   flowers**

1. My friend lives in a _____ on Orleans Terrace.

2. Children like the _____ at the party.

3. In the spring, _____ grown everywhere.

4. You have to _____ the pasta before you can eat it.

PRACTICE THE "OW" SOUND

 (Play Track 69)

43.3 The "ow" produces two sounds. One has the long / ō / sound and the other the /ow/ sound. For example, the word "know" has the long o sound, while the word "now" has the /ow/ sound. Listen and repeat the words that have the long o sound.

Long o

Below	Show	Bowl	Own
Throw	Grow	Elbow	Rows
Mow	Snow	Follow	Tow
Slow	Borrow	Low	Yellow

Let's practice the words that have the / ow / sound. Listen and repeat.

How	Plow	Towel	Allow
Now	Powder	Tower	Bowels
Shower	Somehow	Vowel	Crowd
Clown	Down	Wow	Brown

CONVERSATION PRACTICE

 (Play Track 70)

43.4 Listen to the conversation and repeat. Then, practice with a partner.

Willow: Hi, Woodrow. Do you know if it will snow tonight?

Woodrow: I hope not, Willow. I don't like to plow snow.

Willow: I know. It snowed thirty-three inches last winter. Somehow, it slows me down.

Woodrow: Wow. I didn't know that much snow fell last year.

Willow: Now I hear even more is coming!

Woodrow: Let's hope not too much comes down.

43.5 The double o (oo) makes more than one sound. One like in the word ***noon***, and one like in the word ***book***. Listen and repeat the words. Write them in the correct column.

Supplemental Component p. 167

 (Play Track 71)

room	foot	neighborhood
pool	hook	look
food	tool	cartoon
took	balloon	shook
wood	soon	broom
too	cook	brook

"oo" that sounds like "noon"

1. _____
2. _____
3. _____
4. _____
5. _____
6. _____
7. _____
8. _____
9. _____

"oo" that sounds like "book"

1. _____
2. _____
3. _____
4. _____
5. _____
6. _____
7. _____
8. _____
9. _____

MORE READING PRACTICE

Meet Willow.

43.6 Read the story and answer the questions with complete sentences.

> Willow is a young woman from South Korea. She moved to New York in 2024 to study engineering. She likes New York, but doesn't like the cold weather. Where she lives, it snows a lot. The roads can be very dangerous when they are covered with ice. Willow stays home when there is too much snow outside. She likes New York better in the spring and summer months.

Write the answers to the questions in complete sentences on the lines.

For example: Where is Willow from? She is from South Korea.

1. Where did Willow move? _____

2. What does Willow do when it snows a lot? _____

_____

3. Why did Willow move to New York? _____

4. Willow says she does not like cold weather. Do you like cold weather? Tell me why.

_____

_____

DO YOU LIKE MONEY?

What should you do with it?

MONEY: COINS  (Play Track 72)

44. Look at the different coins and their values. Listen and repeat.

1. a penny
one cent

2. a nickel
five cents

3. a dime
ten cents

4. a quarter
twenty-five cents

5. a half-dollar
fifty cents

6. a dollar coin
one dollar

44.1 How much is it? Can you figure out the value for the following?

For example: *How much is three pennies and three dimes?* __33 ¢__

Supplemental
Component
p. 168

1. How much is one penny, two nickels, and one quarter? _____
2. How much is two quarters, one dime, and three nickels? _____
3. How much is one half-dollar, three dimes, and one penny? _____
4. How much is one dollar coin, three nickels, one dime, and seven pennies? _____
5. How much is three quarters, four dimes, one nickel, and six pennies? _____
6. How much is two half-dollars, four quarters, and ten dimes? _____

MONEY: BILLS

 (Play Track 73)

44.2 Look at the different dollar bills. Listen and repeat.

1. one dollar bill
   one dollar ($1)

2. five dollar bill
   five dollars ($5)

3. ten dollar bill
   ten dollars ($10)

4. twenty dollar bill
   twenty dollars ($20)

5. fifty dollar bill
   fifty dollars ($50)

6. one hundred dollar bill
   one hundred dollars
   ($100)

How much is......?

For example:

6 x $5 = $30

2 x $5 + 1 x $10 = $20

1. 3 x $5 = _____

2. 9 x $1 = _____

3. 6 x $10 = _____

4. 13 x $1 + 1 x $5 = _____

5. 2 x $50 + 2 x $1 = _____

6. 3 x $100 = _____

7. 2 x $20 + 4 x $5 = _____

8. 1 x $50 + 4 x $10 = _____

9. 17 x $1 + 2 x $5 = _____

10. 6 x $20 = _____

11. 3 x $20 + 1 x $10 = _____

12. 1 x $1 + 2 x $5 + 3 x $10 +

    4 x $20 + 1 x $50 = _____

HOW MUCH IS IT?

44.3 When you ask "how much," you ask for the total cost of something. Look at the prices of the food items below. Then add up the total of the combinations in questions 1-6.

Fresh Menu

Pizza
$2.50

Hamburger
$5.00

Turkey Sub
$6.50

Salad
$8.00

Water
$2.00

Coffee
$1.00

Banana
75¢

Cookie
$1.00

1. How much is 1 pizza and 1 bottled water? _____

2. How much is 1 turkey sub, 1 bottled water and 1 cookie? _____

3. How much is 2 hamburgers, 2 bottled waters and 1 banana? _____

4. How much is 1 salad and 2 coffees? _____

5. How much is 1 pizza, 1 hamburger, 2 cookies and 2 bottled waters? _____

6. How much is 1 hamburger, 1 salad, 1 bottled water, 1 coffee and 2 bananas?

_____

44.4 What is the different between HOW MUCH and HOW MANY?

- Both ask about the quantity of something. You use HOW MUCH with money and weight. For example, you can ask "How much does it cost?" or "How much water do you want?"

- You use HOW MANY with individual items that can be counted. For example, you can say "How many students are in class?" or "How many hours did you work last week?"

Complete the following sentences using either MUCH or MANY. For example:

How __many__ cars are there?

How __much__ is this computer?

Then, match them with the correct response.

1. How _____ money do you need? _____	a. There are nine women.
2. How _____ TVs are in your house? _____	b. It is $20.
3. How _____ is your light bill? _____	c. I want three pizzas.
4. How _____ is it? _____	d. You should sleep eight hours.
5. How _____ are the shoes? _____	e. I need $100.
6. How _____ women are in class? _____	f. I worked 35 hours last week.
7. How _____ food do you want? _____	g. There are six in my house.
8. How _____ days are you here? _____	h. My light bill is $72.
9. How _____ sleep do you need? _____	i. The shoes are $12.
10. How _____ hours did you work? ____	j. I am here for seven days.

CONVERSATION PRACTICE

 (Play Track 74)

44.5 Listen to the following short conversation and repeat.
Then, practice with a partner.

Audrey: Hi, Troy. I was wondering, how much lemonade should I bring to the party?

Troy: Hello, Audrey. Well, we will have twenty people from Homestead at the party. You should bring three to four gallons. They love sweet lemonade.

Audrey: How many people?

Troy: There should be twenty people or more.

Audrey: Wow. Should I bring food, too?

Troy: Sure! Will you cook good food for the party?

Audrey: Yes, I will. I love to cook many kinds of food. I think I will bring grilled shrimp with a lime twist.

Troy: Excellent. Everyone will enjoy that!

Answer the following questions about the conversation above.

1. How much lemonade should Audrey bring to the party? _____

2. How many people will be at the party? _____

3. Where are the people from? _____

4. What will Audrey bring to the party? _____

5. Will Audrey bring food?   A) Yes, she will.   B) No, she won't.

FOOD: PERISHABLE AND NON-PERISHABLE

45. There are two main types of food: perishable and non-perishable. Perishable foods are foods that can "spoil" or "go bad" after a short period of time. These foods generally have expiration dates. These dates can be found on the packages they are sold in. However, fresh fruits and vegetables are considered perishable foods and people understand they will spoil in a matter of days. Other types of foods spoil faster if they

Apples   Lettuce   Tomatoes

Foods like apples, lettuce and tomatoes will rot or "spoil" if you don't eat them within a certain amount of days.

Chicken is also known as "poultry"   Cheese

Foods like milk, chicken, and cheese are also perishable. These foods have "expiration dates" and must be kept in refrigeration until they are to be cooked or eaten. Some other foods that should be kept in the refrigerator include:

Fish   meat   orange juice   eggs

NON-PERISHABLE FOOD

Supplemental
Component
p. 169

45.1 Some foods do not spoil for a long time. Others do not need to go into the refrigerator. These foods come in different containers. The containers have Labels on them known as "expiration dates." These dates are either below, Next to, or under the phrase "Best if used by." Look at the examples.

SEP 28 2027

BEST IF USED BY

(A)

BEST BY   06 DEC

NET WT 20 OZ (1 LB 4 OZ)
567g

(B)

Best if used by
09/09/26
B 5252A

Packaged in
Recycled
Paperboard

(C)

Look at the labels and answer the following questions.

1. What is the expiration date of label (A)? _____
2. What is the expiration date of label (B)? _____
3. What is the expiration date of label (C)? _____

45.2   Examples of non-perishable foods include the following:

Discussion

Canned Vegetables   Canned Beans   Box of Cereal   Pasta   Juice Box

Can you list other non-perishable foods? _____

_____

_____

HEALTHY OR UNHEALTHY?

45.3 Do you know what healthy foods are? Look at the foods below. Which are good for your body?

Which is healthier? A fruit salad? Or a piece of chocolate cake?

Although the cake is a delicious, sweet dessert, it is very fattening and high in sugar and cholesterol. Fruit salad has vitamins and nutrients which are good for your body. That's why the fruit salad is much healthier for you. Now, look at the following foods. Put a check by the foods you think are healthy.

hamburger and french fries

Fresh Vegetables

Candy

Avocado

Ice Cream

Water

121

THE PRESENT PROGRESSIVE TENSE (PRESENT CONTINUOUS)

46. We use the *Present Progressive* (also known as Present Continuous) with normal verbs to express something that is happening at the moment. We add -ing at the end of the verb to indicate the progressive tense. Look at the following examples:

I am listening.

He is reading.

They are watching TV.

He is learning English now.

Remember verb + ing = present continuous. For example, *go + ing = going*

Affirmative Statements	Negative Statements	Questions
I am going.	I am not going.	Am I going?
She is working.	She isn't working.	Is she working?
They are talking.	They aren't talking.	Are they talking?
You are eating.	You aren't eating.	Are you eating?
It is flying.	It isn't flying.	Is it flying?

Write -*ing* at the end of the verbs to make them progressive. For example: Look *Looking*

1. walk _____

2. try _____

3. sleep _____

4. kneel _____

5. wear _____

6. sing _____

7. cook _____

8. think _____

46.1 Complete the following sentences using the progressive tense. Use the verb in parenthesis. Some are negative, so remember to use contractions.

1. Manuel is _____ home today. (stay)

2. Charley and Sharon _____ TV. (are not watch)

3. Tony is _____ the hotel. (guard)

4. Sam _____ a house. (is not build)

5. Thelma and Chuck are _____ sick people. (help)

6. Rosita's Restaurant is _____ for waiters. (look)

7. We _____ the Internet right now. (are not

   search)

8. Eva is _____ candy at the store. (buy)

9. Mr. Quinn _____ juice. (is not drink)

Supplemental
Component
p. 170

46.2 Rewrite the following sentences in the present progressive tense. Remember to drop the -s and put the -ing. Some verbs will need a "helping verb" (is, are, and am).

For example: She eats pizza.   She *is eating* pizza.

1. He wears a hat.   _____

2. Eva visits her mother.   _____

3. They go to class.   _____

4. She talks on the phone.   _____

5. We drink water.   _____

6. I work on Saturday.   _____

7. Snow falls down.   _____

IDENTIFYING CLOTHES AND COLORS

 (Play Track 75)

47. Look at the pictures. Listen and repeat.

First, let's identify the colors.

1. White
2. Red
3. Blue
4. Yellow
5. Brown
6. Black
7. Green
8. Purple

Next, let's identify men's clothes.

14. Jacket

9. Shirt
10. Tie
11. Belt
12. Pants
13. Shoes

Now, let's identify women's clothes.

15. Blouse
16. Dress
17. Purse
18. High Heels
19. Glasses
20. Bracelet

CONVERSATION PRACTICE

 (Play Track 76)

47.1 Listen to the conversation and repeat. Then, practice with a partner. Look at pictures 1, 2, and 3 and change the underlined words to make them true.

A: What color <u>is her dress</u>?

B: <u>It's blue.</u>

A: What color <u>are her shoes</u>?

B: <u>They're white.</u>

1.

2.

3.

Now, look around and see what others are wearing. What are your classmates wearing? What is your teacher wearing? Can you name the colors? Write three sentences about what your classmates are wearing.

For example: *Sam is wearing a green shirt.*

1. _____

2. _____

3. _____

Supplemental component p. 171

UNIT 4: COMPREHENSION CHECK (Play Track 77)

48. Listen to the conversations and circle the answers to the questions.

1. What is the woman looking for? A) bowls   B) towers   C) towels

2. How much money does the man have? A) 35 cents   B) 75 cents   C) 45 cents

3. How much money does the man have? A) $30   B) $40   C) $50

4. Does the woman have enough money for
   the three sandwiches? A) yes   B) no

5. Which of the following sentences is in
   the present progressive tense?
   A) She eats pizza.
   B) She is eating pizza.
   C) She will eat pizza.

6. Which of the following sentences is in
   the future tense?
   A) He will buy new shoes.
   B) He is buying new shoes.
   C) He buys new shoes.

7. What color shirt does the man want to get
   for his father?
   A) green   B) purple   C) white

8. What is the woman looking for?
   A) a party
   B) a new dress
   C) Saturday night

9. What does the man want to eat?
   A) something healthy
   B) a hamburger
   C) something cheaper

9

126

MAJOR HOLIDAYS

Americans celebrate many holidays.

49. These are some holidays celebrated in America. Read some facts about them.

1. New Year's Day. January 1st.

> The 1st of January is also the first day of each new year. People around the world celebrate this day to welcome the new year.

2. Valentine's Day. February 14th.

> Valentine's Day is known as the day to express your love for another person. Men and women involved in a romantic relationship usually celebrate this day.

3. St. Patrick's Day. March 17th.

> St. Patrick's Day is generally known as an Irish holiday celebrating St. Patrick for introducing Christianity to Ireland, but it is also an Irish cultural celebration.

4. Easter. Between March 22 and April 25th.

> Easter is a Christian holiday celebrating the resurrection of Jesus Christ. People usually associate Easter with springtime themes like flowers, rabbits, and painted eggs.

5. **Memorial Day**. The last Monday in May.

Memorial Day is a day to remember soldiers who died while serving in the United States military.

6. Independence Day. The 4th of July.

On the 4th of July, 1776, the Declaration of Independence was signed. Americans honor the 4th of July every year as a celebration of independence from Great Britain and to express American pride.

7. **Labor Day**. First Monday in September.

Labor Day recognizes the hard working men and women of the United States. It also marks the last weekend of the summer.

8. Halloween. October 31st.

Halloween is a tradition that comes from Ireland that started over 2,000 years ago. Children wear costumes and adults give out candy when they knock saying "Trick or Treat" in the late evening on October 31st.

9. **Thanksgiving**. Fourth Thursday in November.

People celebrate Thanksgiving throughout the United States as a day for family and friends to share a big meal together and give thanks for the good things in their lives.

10. *Christmas*. December 25th.

Christmas is a religious holiday that comes at the end of each year. Christians around the world mark this day as the birthday of Jesus Christ.

HOLIDAY QUIZ

49.1 Answer the following questions about the 10 holidays from Section 49.

1. What holiday started in Ireland over 2,000 years ago?

_____

2. What holiday do Americans celebrate independence from Great Britain?

_____

3. On what day do people celebrate Valentine's Day?

_____

4. What holiday do people celebrate on December 25th?

_____

5. What holiday remembers soldiers who died while serving in the United States military?

_____

6. What holiday do people celebrate by sharing a big meal with family and friends?

_____

7. What holiday celebrates the first day of a new year?

_____

8. What holiday comes the first Monday in September?

_____

9. What holiday do Christians celebrate between March 22nd and April 25th?

_____

10. On what day do people celebrate St. Patrick's Day?

_____

49.2 Write about two holidays celebrated in the country you are from.

1

Name of a holiday from your country:

_____

What does this holiday celebrate?

_____

How do you celebrate this holiday?

_____

_____

2

Name of holiday from your country:

_____

What does this holiday celebrate?

_____

How do you celebrate this holiday?

_____

_____

SAFETY SIGNS  (Play Track 78)

50. Signs have important information. They can give directions or tell us something is dangerous. Look at the signs below. Listen and repeat.

1. Do not enter.

2. Caution. Wear Safety Goggles When Using Equipment

3. Danger. Poison.

4. Flammable

5. Emergency Exit

6. Danger. High Voltage.

7. No Smoking

8. Caution. Wet Floor

9. First Aid

50.1 What do the signs mean? Look at the signs from Section 50. Match the descriptions with the correct signs.

a.

1. Do not drink this. It will make you very sick or even kill you. _____

b.

2. If you are not careful walking through this hallway, you may fall down. _____

c.

3. You are not allowed to enter here.
_____

d.

4. If you are hurt, you can find bandages and ice packs here. _____

e.

5. You might start a fire with this. _____

f.

6. Please leave the building through here in an emergency. _____

7. To use this equipment, you will need to wear these. _____

g.

8. You are not allowed to smoke here.
_____

h.

9. You may be electrocuted in this area.
_____

i.

50.2 Look at pictures 1, 2, and 3. What do you think they mean?
Turn and talk with a partner about these pictures.

Discussion

1.

2.

3.

 (Play Track 79)

50.3 Listen to the short conversations. Then match the safety sign that goes with
each conversation and circle either A, B, or C. You will hear everything two times.

1. Which sign are the men talking about?

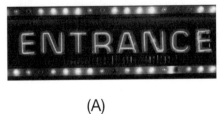

(A)

(B)

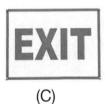

(C)

2. Which sign are the men talking about?

(A)

(B)

(C)

51. UNIT 4 ASSESSMENT  (Play Track 80)

Part 1:

Look at the pictures and listen. Circle the correct answer. Is the correct answer *A*, *B*, or *C*?

1.

(A)   (B)   (C)

2.

(A)   (B)   (C)

Part 2

Listen to the conversations. Listen again and answer the questions. You will hear everything two times.

Use this answer sheet.

Drill #1

1. How much are the bananas?

2. How many people are at the restaurant?

3. Which food is healthy?

Drill #2

4. What holiday is it?

5. What is the teacher wearing?

6. What is the man doing?

Unit 4:

Listening Drills 1 and 2

Circle the best answer to the questions.

For example: A   B

1. A   B   C

2. A   B   C

3. A   B   C

4. A   B   C

5. A   B   C

6. A   B   C

SUPPLEMENTAL ACTIVITIES

Units 1-4 have lessons which students may need more help with. The following activities complement the units.

PRACTICE SAYING THE FOLLOWING SEQUENCE OF LETTERS.

1.	2.	3.

C - a - t   C - i - t - y   P - l - a - n - e

4.	5.	6.

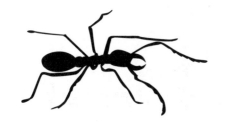  

A - n - t   T - a - b - l - e   S - e - a - t - s

7.	8.	9.

M - a - n   G - i - r - l   H - o - u - s - e

PRACTICING SHORT VOWELS

Look at the pictures and say the words. These will help you remember how to pronounce the short vowels.

A   E   I   O   U

Cat
/ a /

Bed
/ e /

Six
/ i /

Mop
/ o /

Sun
/ u /

Man
/ a /

Red Lips
/ e /   / i /

Dog
/ o /

Cup
/ u /

PRACTICING NUMBERS

Look at the pictures and answer the questions with the best answer.

1. How many people are there?

   a. ten
   b. eleven
   c. nine

2. How many soccer balls are there?

   a. ten
   b. three
   c. eight

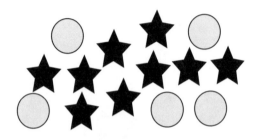

3. How many stars are there?

   a. nine
   b. thirteen
   c. thirty

4. How many planes are there?

   a. eleven
   b. twelve
   c. thirteen

Practice spelling the following numbers and pronouncing them on your own.

1. 60 __ __ __ __ __

2. 11 __ __ __ __ __ __

3. 20 __ __ __ __ __ __

4. 13 __ __ __ __ __ __ __ __

5. 7 __ __ __ __ __

6. 15 __ __ __ __ __ __ __

7. 90 __ __ __ __ __ __

8. 17 __ __ __ __ __ __ __ __ __

9. 70 __ __ __ __ __ __ __

Match the numbers with their spelling. For example:

Two ⟷ 2

1. Eleven
2. Twenty
3. Thirteen
4. Thirty
5. Seven
6. Five
7. One hundred
8. Forty
9. Seventy
10. 50
11. 15
12. 4
13. 8
14. 19
15. 0
16. 9
17. 90
18. 12

a. nineteen
b. twelve
c. 40
d. four
e. 5
f. fifty
g. 7
h. eight
i. nine
j. ninety
k. 11
l. 20
m. 13
n. 30
o. fifteen
p. 100
q. 70
r. zero

Write the numbers using the dash. For example: 21   _twenty-one_

19.   23   _____

20.   31   _____

21.   55   _____

22.   99   _____

Section 5 SPELLING

Fill in the missing vowel to complete the words and sentences. Then practice saying the words. Remember your vowels: / a /   / e /   / i /   / o /   / u /

For example: My n _a_ me is S _a_ m.

1. H___llo. What ___s your n___me?
2. N___ce to meet you. I ___m Sam.
3. How do you sp___ll your n___me?
4. T ___ll me your l ____ st name.
5. Wh ____ t is your f ____ rst name?

Numbers. Spell the following numbers on the line.

1. 7   _____

2. 12   _____

3. 20   _____

4. 19   _____

5. 8   _____

6. 16   _____

7. 9   _____

8. 14   _____

9. 70   _____

10. 90   _____

Section 8   Vocabulary Focus: Words with short / ŏ / and / ē /.

What do these words mean?

When you cross the street, you walk across the white lines on the corner of the street. This is a ***crosswalk***.

This is a ***stoplight***. When the light turns red, cars have to stop. Green signals to go, and yellow means for cars to slow down and prepare to stop.

This is a ***mailbox***. You send letters here.

This is the ***post office***. You mail packages and letters here.

More vocabulary words from Section 8.

This is a **building**. Some are big and some are small.

This is a **convenience store**. You find these near your house. You can buy many things in a convenience store.

Fast Mart

This is a **street**. Cars drive on streets in the city.

This is a **flea market**. Here people buy and sell goods.

PREPOSITIONS OF PLACE

on	between	across from
next to	on the corner of	in back of
behind	in front of	near

Practice pronouncing each preposition and prepositional phrase.

On

The cup is <u>on</u> the table.

Next to

The boy is <u>next to</u> the dog.

Behind / in back of

The cat is <u>behind</u> the tree.

The cat is <u>in back of</u> the tree.

Between

The baby is <u>between</u> the man and the woman.

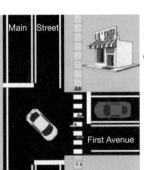

On the corner of

The store is <u>on the corner of</u> Main Street and First Avenue.

In front of

The chicken is <u>in front of</u> the car.

145

Around the City: Look at each direction and label the map correctly. Look carefully at the clues. Number one is done for you.

1. The school is across from the park.
2. The clinic is across from the mechanic shop.
3. The supermarket is next to the mechanic shop.
4. The church is on the corner of U Avenue and Main Street.
5. The fire station is across from Tom's Pizza.
6. The soccer field is next to the school.
7. The gas station is on the corner of T Avenue and Main Street.
8. The bus stop is between the park and the hospital.
9. The pharmacy is next to the clinic.

Tom's Pizza

T Avenue ___ ___ ___   ___ ___ ___

Main Street

Mechanic Shop

U Avenue ___ ___ ___   ___ ___ ___

School

Parking Lot   Police Station

V Avenue ___ ___ ___   ___ ___

Park   BUS STOP   Hospital

BEFORE, AFTER, BETWEEN

Look at the following examples.

 1 is before 2.

 9 is after 8.

6 is between 5 and 7.

Answer the following questions using *before*, *after*, or *between*.

1. What number is **after** eleven? _____

2. What number is **before** forty-six? _____

3. What number is **after** seventeen? _____

4. What number is **before** twenty-two? _____

5. What number is **before** ninety-one? _____

6. What number is **after** seventy-four? _____

7. What number is **between** five and seven? _____

8. What number is **after** two hundred six? _____

9. What number is **before** one hundred eighteen? _____

Answer the following questions using before, after or between.

Example: **Rick is <u>before</u> Pat.**

1. Jill is _____ Jack.

2. Jack is _____ Rick.

3. Rick is _____ Jill and Pat.

4. Pat is _____ Rick

5. Jill is _____ Jack and _____ Rick.

6. Rick is _____ Jill.

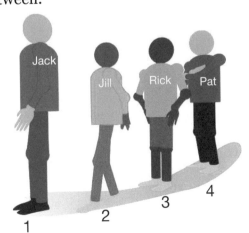

* * People standing in line.

PREPOSITION OF PLACE USING NUMBERS

D

Write the answers on the line. For example: What number is after two? ___*three*___

1. What number is between three and one? _____

2. What number is before seven? _____

3. What number is after twelve? _____

4. What number is between twenty-one and twenty-three? _____

5. What number is before thirty-four? _____

6. What number is after fifty-seven? _____

Look at the group of people and answer the questions that follow.

1	2	3	4	5	6
Peter	Mary	Paul	Yosef	Julie	Kim

*** *There may be more than one answer possible.* ***

1. Where is Paul? _____

2. Mary is _____ Peter and Paul.

3. Julie is _____

4. Peter is _____

5. Kim is _____

6. Yosef is _____

Section 14   Read the stories below. Find the words with digraphs and fill in the blanks.

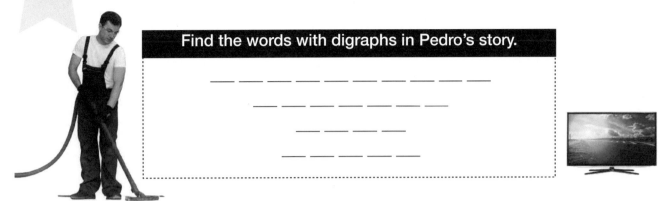

Find the words with digraphs in Pedro's story.

___ ___ ___ ___ ___ ___ ___ ___

___ ___ ___ ___ ___ ___

___ ___ ___ ___ ___

___ ___ ___ ___ ___

Pedro's Story

Hello. My name is Pedro. I live in Washington. I work for Thunder Cleaners. I go to work at 5:00 AM. I leave work at 6:00 PM. I like my job. When I get home, I like to cook and watch TV.

Find the words with digraphs in Mary's story.

___ ___ ___ ___ ___ ___ ___ ___ ___ ___ ___ ___

___ ___ ___ ___

___ ___ ___ ___ ___ ___

___ ___ ___ ___

Mary's Story

Hi. I'm Mary. I live in Philadelphia. I like to sing and dance. I also like to whistle when I walk.

WHO?

*"**Who**"* is a that has the digraph *WH*, but does not make the / w / sound like other words with *WH*. "Who" is pronounced with the h sound.

Who is Chuck?   **Who is that?**   **Who are you?**

Look at the pictures below and read the sentences. Each sentence names and describes one of the pictures. Match them and write their names in the boxes under the pictures.

1. Who is Sam? Sam is the construction worker. He is working now.

2. Who is Felix? Felix is a black cat.

3. Who is Abel? Abel is the young man wearing glasses.

4. Who is Debra? Debra is the woman with black hair.

5. Who is Oscar? Oscar is wearing a hat. He is from Guatemala.

A pronoun is a word that takes the place of a noun (like the name of a person). For example, you can say:

> David is home. David is reading a blog.

Pronouns can replace names so you do not have to repeat them. In the example above, we can change **David** to "**he**."

> David is home. He is reading a blog.

"He" takes the place of "David."

Common singular pronouns include: **I, you, she, it**

Common plural pronouns include: **we, you, they**

***Note: "You" can be used for both singular or plural, but the "to be" verb "**are**" is always used even when using "you" as a singular pronoun. For example: You **are** my friend. (**singular**)   You **are** my friends. (**plural**)*

Rewrite the following sentences by changing the <u>underlined</u> word or words to pronouns.

1. <u>Sam</u> calls Eva every day.

_____

2. <u>Thelma and Phillip</u> work at a hospital.

_____

3. <u>Heather</u> is from Philadelphia.

_____

4. <u>Charley and Sharon</u> are students.

_____

5. <u>Chuck</u> is a doctor.

_____

6. <u>Sharon and I</u> are in school.

_____

Section 18.2

A

Let's review the simple present tense and the verb "to be."

Write the correct verbs to complete the sentences. Remember to use *is*, *are* and *am*.

For example: Sam _is_ from Baltimore.

1. Mary and John _____ friends.

2. Thelma _____ between Heather and Charley.

3. I _____ from Washington.

4. Sharon _____ near the beach.

5. There _____ three teachers in the pharmacy.

6. They _____ in front of the hospital.

7. We _____ in class now.

8. He _____ friends with Charley.

9. The doctors _____ from Manchester.

10. Phillip _____ next to Thelma.

Now let's practice completing the following sentences using is, are, and am + plus the correct preposition (next to, between, on, and near).

1. The man _____ the chair.

2. The man_____ the elephant and the shopping cart.

3. The chicken_____ the elephant.

4. The elephant_____ the man.

152

MORE PRACTICE: USING PREPOSITIONS AND VERB "TO BE."

Complete the sentences using phrases from the list.

is between	are near	is in front of
is on	am next to	

The car _____ the house.

2. The computer _____ the man and woman.

3. They _____ the water.

4. The money _____ the table.

5. I _____ the bicycle.

Section 18.3 HOW DO YOU FEEL?

Feelings are adjectives. Adjectives are words that describe nouns. Look at the pictures. Each picture has a feeling describing it. For example:

She is happy.
*She **feels** happy.*

1.

2.

3.

She is sad.	He is angry.	She is sick.
You can also say:		
She feels sad.	**He feels angry.**	**She feels sick.**

Look at these pictures. How do they feel?

(A) She feels sleepy.

(B) She feels hungry.

(A) She feels happy.

(B) She feels tired.

Now, it's your turn. How do you feel? Complete the following sentences, then write one on your own.

1. At home I feel _____.

2. In class I feel _____.

3. _____

PRACTICE TELLING TIME.

Look at the pictures. Circle the time
you think it is.

1. A) 12:00 PM   B) 7:00 PM   C) 11:00 PM

2. A) 8:00 AM   B) 12:45 PM   C) 9:45 PM

3. A) 1:00 PM   B) 8:30 PM   C) 3:00 AM

4. A) 8:00 PM   B) 8:00 AM   C) 2:00 AM

5. A) 11:00 PM   B) 5:00 PM   C) 1:45 AM

Section 19.1 Learning the times of day. Look at the following times and write what time of day they are in. For example: 3:00PM <u>in the afternoon</u>

1. 12:10 PM _____

2. 4:45 PM _____

3. 7:01 AM _____

4. 5:46 PM _____

5. 9:30 PM _____

6. 11:55 AM _____

7. 6:36 PM _____

8. 10:15 PM _____

9. 2:05 PM _____

Match the times with the *times of day*. For example:

8:00AM ←——————————→ in the morning

- 7:00 PM   * in the afternoon

- 12:00PM   * at night

- 5:00 AM   * Midnight

- 2:00 PM   * Noon

- 10:00 PM   * in the morning

- 12:00AM   * in the evening

156

Section 20   Look at the pictures and answer the questions. Use the guide in Section 20 to help you. The first one is done for you.

1. Are they in school?   No, they aren't.

2. Are they at the park?

_____

3. Is she happy?

_____

4. Is it 11:54?

_____

5. Is she at lunch?

_____

6. Is the dog near the water?

_____

Section 28.1   Let's practice pronouncing words with the "er" sound / ɜː /.

Common words using the / ɜː / sound.

ur	ir	er	ear	wor
church	*birth*day	nerve	earth	work
hurt	girl	herb	learn	worse
burn	skirt	her	search	worth
curve	first	serve	early	world
nurse	dirt	fern	earn	word

Label the pictures with the correct word.

_____

_____

_____

_____

_____

_____

_____

_____

DAYS OF THE WEEK / MONTHS OF THE YEAR

Match the days with their ordinal number.

Saturday	First
Tuesday	Second
Thursday	Third
Monday	Fourth
Sunday	Fifth
Friday	Sixth
Wednesday	Seventh

Write the ordinal number for each month of the year.

March	_Third_	December	_____
May	_____	July	_____
September	_____	January	_____
October	_____	April	_____
June	_____	February	_____
November	_____	August	_____

Section 29.1   Ordinal Numbers: Complete the missing information. The first two are done for you.

1. First   1st

2. 4th   fourth

3. 15th   _____

4. third   _____

5. 11th   _____

6. twentieth   _____

7. seventh   _____

8. 2nd   _____

9. nineteenth   _____

10. 21st   _____

11. 30th   _____

12. twelfth   _____

---

1. Circle the fourth star from the left.

2. Circle the third cat from the left.

3. Circle the second fish from the right.

   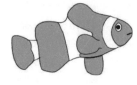 

POSSESSIVE NOUNS

Possessive nouns show who or what something belongs to (another noun), and is represented in the form of apostrophe ('). Most nouns show possession with an (') + s, but others that end in s (because they are plural), simply add the apostrophe ('). Look at the guide below for examples.

Nouns	Apostrophe	Examples
Singular Nouns	add 's	Sam ⟶ Sam's birthday
		boss ⟶ the boss's house
Plural Nouns	add '	the girls ⟶ the girls' soccer team
Plural Nouns (Irregular)	add 's	men ⟶ the men's football team

Rewrite the underlined words to make them possessives.

For example: <u>John</u> mother bakes cookies.   <u>John's</u> mother bakes cookies.

1. <u>Kate</u> sister is in my class.   _____

2. We are at <u>Gus</u> party.   _____

3. The two <u>boys</u> class is in room 201.   _____

4. My friend <u>Luis</u> daughter is here.   _____

5. This is the <u>dog</u> toy.   _____

6. It looks like <u>Barbara</u> car.   _____

7. Are you going to <u>Max</u> wedding?   _____

8. Wendy only cuts <u>women</u> hair.   _____

9. Where is <u>David</u> book?   _____

USING "WILL" AND "WON'T."

Add *will* or *won't* to make the sentences true about you.

For example: I'll buy clothes this weekend.

She will work tomorrow.

My brother won't visit me this weekend.

1. My mother _____ visit me tomorrow.

2. I _____ eat breakfast now.

3. I _____ practice English tonight.

4. I _____ work tomorrow night.

5. My teacher _____ visit Russia tomorrow.

Complete the following sentences using will or won't. Use contractions.

6. (We will) _____ study English tonight.

7. (It will) _____ rain today.

8. (They will not) _____ be in class next Tuesday.

9. (You will) _____ be in New Mexico next week.

10. (He will not) _____ have a birthday party on Sunday.

Match the words with their contractions.   ←————————→

11. I will not   a. We won't

12. You will not   b. She'll

13. He will   c. I won't

14. We will not   d. He'll

15. She will   e. You won't

TO THE FUTURE

Use "will" with another verb to state something you are going to do. Read each sentence. Then, rewrite it in the future tense. Remember to drop the "s" on some verbs. For example:

She helps me.   **_She will help me._**

1. Wayne works tonight.   _____

2. Peter paints six houses.   _____

3. Clory helps sick people.   _____

4. Andrea cuts hair.   _____

5. Chuck works with me.   _____

6. Betty bakes cookies.   _____

7. Eva visits Sam.   _____

8. Tony moves to Arizona.   _____

9. Adesh plays soccer.   _____

10. Brian eats tacos for lunch.   _____

Write four sentences about what you will do in the future.

1._____

2._____

3._____

4._____

CHECK IT OUT!

Read the sentences below. Put a check ✓ mark on the line next to the sentences that are in the future tense.

_____ 1. Pat will eat at Rosita's restaurant.

_____ 2. He loves their tacos.

_____ 3. He will put lots of hot sauce on his tacos.

_____ 4. Sam eats lunch with Eva.

_____ 5. He will order a sandwich.

_____ 6. Eva will order a bowl of pasta.

_____ 7. The woman is looking for the lawyer's office.

_____ 8. Heather will teach math this year.

_____ 9. Charley and Sharon are in Washington today.

_____ 10. They will visit another school later.

_____ 11. Thelma is working at the hospital.

_____ 12. Tomorrow she will help the doctors.

_____ 13. Today she is not working.

_____ 14. Jorge will buy something nice for the party.

_____ 15. This will be his first birthday party in America.

_____ 16. He is looking for new clothes.

_____ 17. I'm trying to find the clinic.

_____ 18. She will show me where to find it.

Section 39.2

Digraphs *KN* and *QU*. Look at the pictures and complete the sentences with the correct word from the box.

queen	knot	know	quarter
knee	knob	squid	knife

1. The cook uses a _____ to cut the onion.

2. She is the _____ of England.

3. Some people like to eat _____.

4. The price of the candy is one _____.

5. I bumped my leg and hurt my _____.

6. The _____ is broken on the door.

7. The _____ is open.

8. Do you _____ the answer?

Section 40.1  Can  Can't

Read each sentence carefully. Complete each sentence using "can" or can't."

1. Mr. Quinn has to work all day. He _____ go to the beach.

2. Tony _____ work on Saturday. He is available.

3. Adesh _____ drive a car. He doesn't have a driver's license.

4. Sam _____ eat too much hot sauce. It will give him stomach problems.

5. Daniel _____ play soccer. His knees hurt.

6. Marcos _____ go to work. He is very sick.

7. Eva _____ go to dinner with Sam on Saturday night. She is going to a concert.

8. Sam _____ help Manuel on Sunday. He is working all weekend.

9. Dogs _____ climb trees.

10. Rabbits _____ run quickly.

11. Please turn on the lights. We _____ see anything.

12. She _____ eat after she is finished working.

13. He hurt his foot so he _____ exercise.

14. Jesus is a singer. He _____ sing many songs.

15. A horse _____ fly.

16. Eva's mother only speaks English. She _____ speak French.

17. Excuse me, Ma'am, _____ you tell me the time?

18. Yes, you _____ take this book home.

Section 43.5 The diphthong "oo" makes multiple sounds, too. Look at the list and practice pronouncing them with your teacher. Then, with a partner.

The following words with the /oo/ make the "oo" sounds like in the word "noon."

food	balloon	mood	boom
smooth	groove	choose	cool
spoon	school	shampoo	boot

The following words with the /oo/ make the "oo" sounds like in the word "cook."

book	took	wood	stood
hook	foot	good	look

Find the words in the puzzle and circle them. Then, practice pronouncing them with a partner.

Words with "OO"

```
X E Q D K H X Z R N H G S D B        TOOL
D L Z X L O R N Q O L M K H C        MOON
Y N C Z O O P P W O L T M Y Z        ROOT
V A X K O E O K L P O O F O H        TOOTH
S F L P Q Q Q S D N O O Q E C        LOOSE
H T D F B K J I E R V T E K N        BATHROOM
A E D Q E K D K H F A H T K N        ZOO
M R Y V D F J T H T W L M U G        SHAMPOO
P N C Y Y X A A O O V Y W C V        POOR
O O U I E B C G I O F R P J O        AFTERNOON
O O V U H X C Y Z R L H F L R
U N E C T M A Y N H Q Q L W R
U Y Z W E H O V W C M C L X Z
T C A A S H L O D P G V Y A J
C A Y U S A B P N B B O I R H
```

Count the coins. Look at each set of coins and write their value.

1. _____

2. _____

3. _____

4. _____

5. _____

Section 45.1   Non-perishable foods. Read the advertisement and answer the questions.

The Fall Food Bank

Help hungry people!
Bring non-perishables to M Street Church

When/Where?

October 9-18
2-7 PM

M Street Church
369 M Street
Washington, D.C 20001

"We feed the hungry."

Help feed hungry families this season by bringing non-perishable foods to M Street Church. Fall marks the start of the holiday season and colder climate. At M Street Church, we wish to warm up homes with bags of food for hungry families that need our help. Help us feed the hungry by donating can foods and other non-perishable items between 2 and 7 PM at the Church. Thank you!

1. What is the advertisement asking for?
   A) any food
   B) non-perishable food
   C) fruit

2. When should you bring the food?
   A) between October 9-18
   B) M Street Church
   C) Washington, D.C.

3. Who is the food for?
   A) M Street Church
   B) Washington, D.C.
   C) hungry families

4. Which of the following foods should you **NOT** bring to the food bank?

(A)

(B)

(C)

5. List any other non-perishable foods for the food bank. _____

_____

_____

Section 46.2 The Present Progressive (Present Continuous). Remember the present progressive are things happening right now. For example, you are **reading** this sentence at this moment. Look at the picture below.

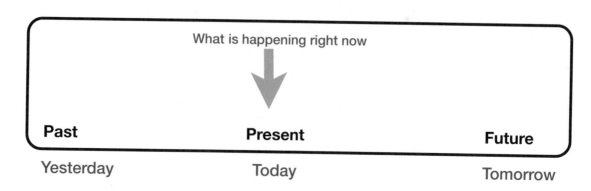

What is happening right now

Past	Present	Future
Yesterday	Today	Tomorrow

In the present progressive, you use the verb "to be" + the -ing verb. For example:

(She eats chocolate.)   She is *eating* chocolate.

Remember to drop the -s on a verb when adding -ing.

Look at the pictures below. What are they doing?

1. (They talk.) _____

2. (They play soccer.) _____

3. (He listens.) _____

4. (She walks home.) _____

5. (It looks at me.) _____

6. (We watch TV.) _____

7. (I read a book.) _____

8. (Sam calls Eva.) _____

9. (You work hard.) _____

Section 47.1 Possessive Pronouns show who (or what) possesses something. Also, a possessive pronoun takes the place of a possessive noun.

> For example: Mary's dress = **her** dress   Juan's car = **his** car
>
>   I own this house. It is **my** house.   She is **your** sister.
>
>   I own these shoes. They are **mine**.   These books are **yours**.
>
>   This is **our** class. The class is **ours**.   It's **their** house. The house is **theirs**.
>
> Other possessive pronouns include: **mine, my, your, yours, its, our, ours, their, theirs**.

Complete the sentences using a pronoun.

1. The book belongs to David. It is _____ book.

2. I paid $50 for the boots. The boots are _____.

3. Adesh and Jorge have a pizza. It is _____ pizza.

4. We live in this house. It is _____ house.

5. This is **my** chair. That is _____ chair.

6. Tomorrow, Sharon turns 60 years old. It is _____ birthday!

7. These papers are **yours**. Those are _____.

8. This TV belongs to Eva. It is _____ TV.

9. Tony works as a security guard. That is _____ job.

10. Manuel's car is very dirty. He needs to clean _____ car.

11. The dogs belong to Ricky and Mike. The dogs are _____.

12. My brother and I have tickets. The tickets are _____.

Map of the 50 States of the United States. The map labels each state and their capitals including the nation's capital.

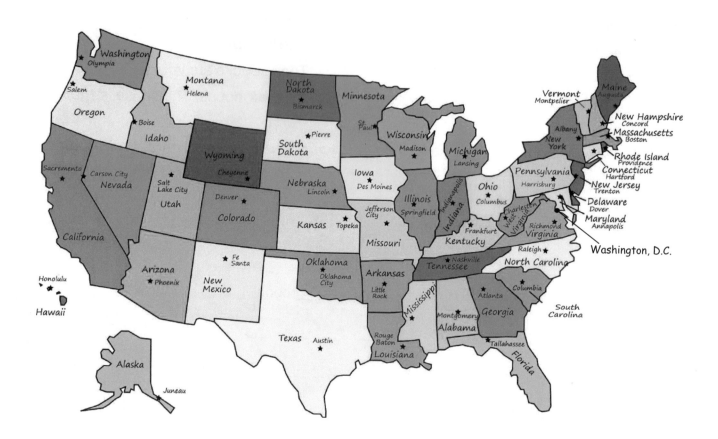

The 50 States in alphabetical order:

Alabama	Indiana	Nebraska	Rhode Island
Alaska	Iowa	Nevada	South Carolina
Arizona	Kansas	New Hampshire	South Dakota
Arkansas	Kentucky	New Jersey	Tennessee
California	Louisiana	New Mexico	Texas
Colorado	Maine	New York	Utah
Connecticut	Maryland	North Carolina	Vermont
Delaware	Massachusetts	North Dakota	Virginia
Florida	Michigan	Ohio	Washington
Georgia	Minnesota	Oklahoma	West Virginia
Hawaii	Mississippi	Oregon	Wisconsin
Idaho	Missouri	Pennsylvania	Wyoming
Illinois	Montana		

PHONICS ASSESSMENTS

Vowel Assessments and Phonics Vocabulary Reference

This section includes:
– *Vowel Pre-Assessment and 1-3*
– *Digraphs*
– *Consonant Blends*
– *Diphthongs*

UNIT 1 VOWELS
ASSESSMENTS

Practice saying the following.

Long Vowels

A	E	I	O	U

Short Vowels

a	e	i	o	u

Practice the following words that have long vowels.

cake	hi	fee	low
huge	rate	lake	right
no	see	day	you

Practice the following words that have short vowels.

hat	get	it	hot
up	not	at	big
yet	cut	bet	cab

LONG / SHORT VOWELS

Listen to your teacher say these words and repeat them. Focus on the long vowel sounds.

1. / a /	Plane	Late	Pain	Spain	Train
2. / e /	Green	Feel	Feet	Ear	See
3. / i /	Right	Bite	Light	Ice	Night
4. / o /	No	Slow	Go	Soap	Boat
5. / u /	You	Fume	Use	Mule	New

Listen to your teacher say these words and repeat them. Focus on the short vowel sounds.

1. / a /	Apple	Ask	Map	Gas	Cat
2. / e /	Bed	Leg	Pen	Red	Wet
3. / i /	Him	Fit	Hit	Is	Pig
4. / o /	Hot	Mop	God	Top	Pot
5. / u /	Bus	Fun	Gum	Sun	Cup

Name _____   Date _____

Long and Short Vowel Pre-Assessment (Practice)

Listen to your teacher say the words in the box. If the word has a *long* vowel sound, write the word in the box under "Long Vowels." If the word has a *short* vowel sound, write the word in the box under "Short Vowels."

Pay	Street	Ice	No	Use
Hat	Head	Sit	Not	Up

Long Vowels

_____

_____

_____

_____

_____

Short Vowels

_____

_____

_____

_____

For the instructor: How many did the student get correct? Use this data to help you formulate emphasis on those vowels students need more help differentiating.

_____
10

Name _____   Date _____

UNIT 1: VOWEL ASSESSMENT 1

Listen to your teacher say the words in the box. If the word has a long vowel sound, write the word in the box under "Long Vowels." If the word has a short vowel sound, write the word in the box under "Short Vowels."

ran	rain	hen	heat	sit	file
not	nope	cut	cute	paid	egg
ice	jog	us	cage	heal	win
leg	fat	an	feel	coat	fight

Long Vowels   Short Vowels

To the instructor: How many did this student get correct? Use this data to help you formulate more emphasis on the those vowels students are having trouble discriminating.

_____
24

Name _____   Date _____

UNIT 1: VOWEL ASSESSMENT 2

Listen to your teacher say the words in the box. If the word has a long vowel sound, write the word in the box under "Long Vowels." If the word has a short vowel sound, write the word in the box under "Short Vowels."

hot	kiss	boat	cake	ice
egg	hear	blind	hat	shake
cup	cat	cream	head	home

Long Vowels (8)   Short Vowels (7)

Listen and circle the words with the short vowel sound. There is only one for each number.

1.   red   find   real

2.   shine   sign   sin

3.   hop   hope   home

4.   fish   fine   fire

5.   cute   cure   cup

20

Name _____   Date _____

UNIT 1: VOWEL ASSESSMENT 3

Part 1:

Practice the conversation. Remember to pronounce long and short vowels correctly.

Student A:	Is there a mechanic shop near here?	Scale 1-10
Student B:	Yes. There is one between the gas station and the parking lot.	(see rubric)
Student A:	Okay. Thank you.	
Student B:	You are welcome.	_____

Part 2:

Directions: If the word has a long vowel, place a line over the word. For example: i̶c̶e̶

If the word has a short vowel, place a ᵘ over the word. For example: hŏt

Listen to your teacher say the words in the box. Then place a — or a ᵘ over the word to show they are either long or short vowels.

shop	gas	lot	tray	yes
here	is	thank	you	there

Part 3:

Listen and circle the words with the short vowel sound. There is only one for each number.

1. please   red   hi
2. up   no   day
3. flea   think   I
4. we   pen   street
5. ride   phone   bus

25

UNIT 2 DIGRAPHS

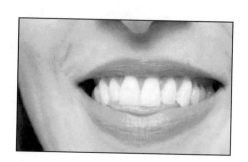

ASSESSMENTS

Assess pronunciation of the following.

Digraphs

TH   SH   CH   PH   NG   WH

Practice words with **voiceless** *TH*

Beginning	*Middle*	*End*
Thin	Toothbrush	Tooth
Thursday	Birthday	Bath
Thank you	Something	Moth

Practice words with **voiced** *TH*

Beginning	*Middle*	*End*
The	Together	Breathe
This	Weather	Bathe
There	Mother	Lathe

Practice the words with SH

Beginning	*Middle*	*End*
Shoe	Dishes	Flash
Shop	Fishing	Wish
Short	Washington	Rash

Continued

Practice words with *CH*

Beginning	**Middle**	**End**
Chair	Inches	Beach
Chicken	Ketchup	Lunch
Cherry	Kitchen	Speech

Practice words with *PH*

Beginning	**Middle**	**End**
Photo	Elephant	Photograph
Pharmacy	Graphics	Joseph
Phone	Alphabet	Paragraph

Practice the words with NG

Middle	**End**
Finger	King
Singer	Long
Bingo	Thing

Practice the words with WH

Beginning	**Middle**
What	Anywhere
Why	Somewhere
When	Nowhere

Name _____   Date _____

Look at the following words. Circle the words that have digraphs. (12)

shower	nope	child	mouth	this
new	flea	sing	cash	church
think	here	class	boy	ship
teacher	cool	book	when	shelf

Read the following sentences. Circle the words with the digraphs. Then, practice saying the sentences. (15)

1. Every morning I brush my teeth and take a shower.

2. The bus has four wheels.

3. This is my brother Chad.

4. I am looking for the pharmacy.

5. She works every Thursday in the city.

Complete the sentences using words from the box.

cheese	long	wash	chair

1. The woman has _____ hair.

2. You sit on a _____.

3. I like my sandwich with _____.

4. _____ your hands after using the bathroom.

____
31

UNIT 3 CONSONANT BLENDS
ASSESSMENTS

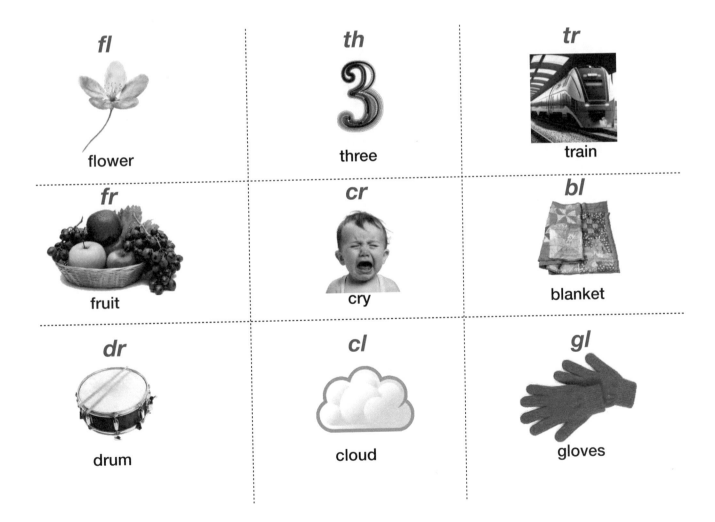

fl	**th**	**tr**
flower	three	train
fr	**cr**	**bl**
fruit	cry	blanket
dr	**cl**	**gl**
drum	cloud	gloves

Name _____   Date _____

Look at each picture. Circle the correct consonant blend that starts each word.

1. fr ch sh   2. shr br pl   3. ch sh th   4. ch sh th

Look at the words in the box below. Complete the sentences with words from the box. Then, practice reading the sentences.

| school   broom   free   glasses   star |

 1. This is a black _____.

2. You need a _____ to sweep the floor.

 3. He needs _____ to read.

4. The children go to _____.

 5.The book costs no money. It is _____.

UNIT 4 DIPHTHONGS

ASSESSMENT

au	**aw**	**ew**	**ow**
haul	raw	new	know
pause	claw	chew	shadow
fault	saw	crew	blow
auto	crawl	interview	bowl
August	law	jewel	flow

oi	**ou**	**oy**	**oo**
boil	out	boy	roof
android	foul	employ	moon
coil	amount	joy	room
point	shout	toy	tool
join	cloud	soy	pool

Name _____   Date _____

Circle the pictures that make the same "oi" sound as in the word "coin." (3)

Practice the conversation. Pay close attention to words with diphthongs. (Scale 1-10)

Student A: Do you know how to cook pasta?

Student B: Yes. You boil the pasta in water and a small amount of salt.

Student A: How long should I boil it?

Student B: For about ten minutes. Drain the water, then put it in a bowl.

Student A: This is good to know. Thank you very much.

Circle the words that have diphthongs. There is only one in each line.

1. this   sauce   hot

2. know   wash   hands

3. straw   vacation   Florida

4. apple   knife   chew

5. what   that   about

	18

Audio Script

Track 1 (1.0)
I Want To Learn English second edition, by Jose V. Torres. Copyright 2024 by the JV Myka Publishing Company. All rights reserved. Section one. Sounding out letters. Let's begin with the English alphabet. Look at each letter as you hear it spoken. Repeat each letter as you hear them.
A. B. C. D. E. F. G. H. I. J. K. L. M. N. O. P. Q. R. S. T. U. V. W. X. Y. Z.

Track 2 (2.0)
Section two. The letters a, e, i, o, and u are called vowels. Vowels produce two sounds. One is called long vowels, and the other is called short vowels. Listen and repeat both long and short vowels. Long vowels: a, e, i, o, u. Short vowels: a, e, I, o, u. Listen and repeat the vowels one more time. (Repeat)

Track 3 (3.0-3.1)
Section three. Let's continue with numbers. Repeat each number as you hear it spoken.
0, 1, 2, 3, 4, 5, 6, 7, 8, 9, 10, 11, 12, 13, 14, 15, 16, 17, 18, 19, 20, 21.
Now, try larger numbers. Listen and repeat.
30, 40, 50, 60, 70, 80, 90, 100, 200, 300, 400, 500, 600, 700, 800, 900, 1000, 10000, 100000, one million.

Track 4 (3.2)
Section 3.2: Now, practice pronouncing the numbers and spelling them from 1 to 20. Then, 30 to 100. I will spell the first ten for you, then practice the rest on your own.
1. O-n-e. 2. T-w-o. 3. T-h-r-e-e. 4. F-o-u-r. 5. F-i-v-e. 6. S-i-x. 7. S-e-v-e-n. 8. E-i-g-h-t. 9. N-i-n-e. 10. T-e-n. Now, practice eleven to one-hundred on your own or with a partner.

Track 5 (3.3)
Section 3.3: Student challenge. Practice numbers from 200 to one million. Two hundred. Three hundred. Four hundred. Five hundred. Six hundred. Seven hundred. Eight hundred. Nine hundred. One thousand. Two thousand. Three thousand. Four thousand. Five thousand. Ten thousand. One hundred thousand. One million.

Track 6 (4.0)
Section four: Learn vocabulary basics. Directions. Listen to the words and repeat. Number one. Listen. Number two. Repeat. Number three. Talk. Number four. Write. Number five. Look. Number six. Point. Number seven. Spell. Number eight. Match.

Track 7 (5.0)
Section five. What is your name? Listen to the recording. Then, practice the short greeting and the spelling of your name. A: Hello. My name is Bella . B: Nice to meet you. I am Schuyler. A: How do you spell your name? B: S-c-h-u-y-l-e-r

Track 8 (6.0)
Section six. Look at the short reading dialogue. Listen to the recording and then repeat. Then, practice with a partner. John: Hello. I am John. Mary: Hello, John. I am Mary. John: Nice to meet you, Mary. Mary: Same here. Nice to meet you, too. Now, listen again and repeat.

Track 9 (6.1)
Section 6.1. Student challenge. Listen and repeat. Practice the conversation with a partner. John: Mary, where is Ray? Mary: Oh, Ray? He is home. John: Will he be here tomorrow? Mary: Yes, he will be here tomorrow. Listen again and repeat.

Track 10 (7.0)
Section seven. Let's review the vowels. Long vowels: a, e, i, o, u. Short vowels: a, e, i, o, u. Practice saying the following words that have the long and short vowels. Able. Read. Ice cream. Boat. Unites States. Now, short vowels. Apple. Eggs. Sit. Pot. Cup. Now, practice saying the long and short vowels on your own. Use the example words to help you. Take the long and short vowel quiz. Use your smart phone camera on the QR code and play the video to test your vowel skills.

Track 11 (8.0)
Section eight. Vowels and vocabulary words. Practice pronunciation. The short vowel /o/. Listen and repeat. Car, far, crosswalk, park, stoplight, mailbox, parking lot, post office. Now practice the long vowel /e/. Listen and repeat. Street, library, building, flea market. Now, practice the pronunciation of some more location words. Listen and mark where you hear the short vowel /o/ or the long vowel /e/. Number one. Check cashing store. Number two. Bank. Number three. Lawyer's office. Number four. Mechanic shop. Number five. Clinic. Number six. Pharmacy. Number seven. Hospital. Number eight. Church. Number nine. Electronic store. Number ten. Gas station. Number eleven. Restaurant. Number twelve. Dentist. Number thirteen. Supermarket. Number fourteen. Convenience store. Number fifteen. Police station.

Track 12 (9.1)
Section 9.1. Around the city. Listen to the short conversations and answer the questions. There may be more than one answer. Number one. Man: What are you looking for, Margaret? Margaret: Well, I have a check that I need to case. Man: Where does Margaret need to go? Number two. Woman: What's wrong, Luis? You look upset. Luis: It's my car. I need to have it fixed. Man: Where should Luis take his car? Number three. Woman: Are you feeling alright? Man: No,

I'm really sick. Man: Where does the man need to go? Number four. Man: Geez, my radio is not working. I need a new radio. Woman: Where should the man go for a new radio? Number five. Man: My friend, Mario, is in real trouble. They're trying to put him in jail. Woman. Wow. He needs a good lawyer. Man: Where should Mario go?

Track 13 (10.0)

Section ten. Around the city. Locations using prepositions. Listen and repeat the words and phrases. On. Next to. Behind. Between. On the corner of. In front of. Across from. In back of. Near.

Track 14 (10.1)

Section 10.1. Do you understand? Look at the map in section 10 and listen to the statements. First, let's do number one together. Listen and answer the questions by circling either A, B or C. Number one. Where is the flea market? A) Fayette Street. B) next to the pharmacy. C) next to Rosita's restaurant. Listen again. (Repeat) The answer is B, next to the pharmacy. Notice "B" is already circled on your answer sheet. This is how you will answer numbers 2 through 7. Now, let's try a few more. Number two. Where is the dentist office? A) next to the bank. B) on the corner of Orleans Terrace and Baltimore Road. C) on the corner of Fayette Street and 83rd Avenue. Let's hear that one more time. (Repeat) Is the answer A, B or C? The answer is "C," on the corner of Fayette Street and 83rd Avenue. Number three. Where is the parking lot? A) between the mechanic shop and the convenience store. B) between the check cashing store and the lawyer's office. C) across from the supermarket. Let's hear that one more time. (Repeat) Is the answer A, B, or C? The answer is "A," between the mechanic shop and the convenience store. Number four. Where is the lawyer's office? A) across from the police station. B) across from the flea market. C) across from the convenience store. Let's hear that one more time. (Repeat) Is the answer A, B, or C? The answer is "B," across from the flea market. Now, let's try some on your own. Listen carefully. You will hear everything two times. Number five. A: Excuse me, I'm looking for the bank. B: It's on Fleet Street, between the supermarket and the check cashing store. A: Thank you. B: You're welcome. What street is the bank on? A) Fayette Street. B) Baltimore Road. C) Fleet Street. Let's hear that one more time.(Repeat) Number six. A: Do you know where the gas station is? B: Yes. There's one on the corner of Orleans Terrace and Fayette Street. Where is the gas station? A) on the corner of Orleans Terrace and Fleet Street. B) on the corner of Orleans Terrace and Fayette Street. C) on the corner of Orleans Terrace and Baltimore Road. Let's hear that one more time. (Repeat) Number seven. A: Excuse me, I'm looking for the pharmacy. B: Oh, the pharmacy is across from the check cashing store. A: You mean the one of Fleet Street? B: Yes, that one. Where is the pharmacy? A) across from the check cashing store. B) on the corner of Fleet Street and Orleans Terrace. C) across from the convenience store. Let's hear that one more time. (Repeat) Listen and answer the following questions on the lines. Number eight. What is next to the dentist office? (Repeat) Number nine. What is between the flea market and the police station? (Repeat) Number ten. What is across from the police station? (Repeat)

Track 15 (11.0)

Section eleven. Around the city. Understanding locations and directions. Listen and read the short conversations. Then, practice with a partner. Sam: Do you know where the flea market is? Pat: Yes. It is on the corner of Fleet Street and 83rd Avenue. Sam: Do you think it is open now? Pat: Maybe. But I am not positive.

Track 16 (11.1)

Section 11.1. Listen to the conversation and then practice with a partner. Sam: I walked around for hours. I am very hungry now. Pat: There is a good restaurant across from the pharmacy and the flea market. Sam: What kind of restaurant is it? Pat: It's a Mexican restaurant. I love their tacos especially with hot sauce. Sam: Hot sauce! Oh, too much hot sauce and I will have stomach problems. Pat: Like I said, the pharmacy is across the street.

Track 17 (12.0)

Section twelve. Unit one assessment. Part two. Listen to the conversation. Listen again and answer the following questions. Drill one. Man: Excuse me. I'm trying to find the clinic. Woman: Well, it's a block away from 83rd Avenue. Man: I don't understand. Woman: If you walk down Fayette Street one more block, it will be on the corner of 83rd Avenue. Man: Thank you very much. Woman: You're welcome. Number one. What is the man looking for? A) 83rd Avenue. B) the clinic. C) the block. Listen to the conversation again. (Repeat) Number two. How far away is the man? A) a mile. B) a block away. C) across the street. Listen to the conversation one more time. (Repeat) Number three. What street is the man on? A) Fayette Street. B) 83rd Avenue. C) Baltimore Street. Listen to the conversation one more time. (Repeat) Drill two. Woman: Hello, sir. Can you help me? Man: How can I help you? Woman: I'm trying to find the lawyer's office. Man: Do you mean the one on Fleet Street? Woman: Yes, that one. Man: It's between 83rd Avenue and Orleans Terrace. Woman: Thank you, sir. Man: And one more thing. It is next to Rosita's Restaurant. Woman: You have been very helpful. Thank you again. Man: No problem. Number four. What is the woman looking for? A) Fleet Street B) 83rd Avenue. C) the lawyer's office. Listen to the conversation again. (Repeat) Number five. On what street is the lawyer's office on? A) 83rd Avenue. B) Orleans Terrace. C) Fleet Street. Listen to the conversation one more time. (Repeat) Number six. What is the lawyer's office next to? A) Rosita's restaurant. B) the convenience store. C) 83rd Avenue.

Track 18 (13.0)

Section thirteen. Digraphs. Let's begin with practicing the pronunciation of digraphs. Listen and repeat. TH /th/ three. SH /sh/ shoe. CH /ch/ chicken. PH /f/ phone. NG /ng/ sing. WH /w/ when.

Track 19 (14.0)

Section fourteen. Look at the pictures and practice saying the words. Whale. Thirteen. Check. Chair. Shoe. These girls. Phone. Ring.

Track 20 (15.0)

Section fifteen. Point to the words that have digraphs and practice by repeating them. Chip. What. Hat. Graph. Think. Wheel. Ship. Hot. Thing. Sit. Long. There.

Track 21 (16.0)
Section sixteen. Listen and repeat the following numbers. Focus on the digraph TH. Three. Thirteen. Thirty. Thirty-one. Thirty-two. Thirty-three. Thirty-four. Thirty-five. Thirty-six. Thirty-seven. Thirty-eight. Thirty-nine. Forty-three. Three hundred. Three hundred thirty-three.

Track 22 (16.2)
Section 16.2. Listen to the sentences and repeat. Focus on the digraphs. Number one. Heather is from Philadelphia. Number two. She is a math teacher. Number three. Charley and Sharon are students.

Track 23 (16.3)
Section 16.3. Practice the conversation. Focus on the digraphs. Phillip: Hi Thelma. Who is Chuck? Thelma: Oh, chuck is the new doctor from Washington. Philip: He's from Washington? Thelma: Yes. One more doctor is coming from Richmond. Phillip: We have thirty-two doctors. One more makes thirty-three. Thelma: That's right. Phillip: How many doctors are in the hospital? Thelma: There are three hundred thirty-three. Phillip: Wow. Thank you for that information, Thelma. Thelma: You're welcome.

Track 24 (19.0)
Section nineteen. Telling time. Look at the time on the clocks. Listen and repeat. Twelve PM. It's twelve o'clock. It's noon. Nine o'clock. It's nine o'clock. Three fifteen. It's three fifteen. It's a quarter after three. Seven thirty. It's seven thirty. It's half past seven. One forty-five. It's one forty-five. It's a quarter to two. Twelve AM. It's midnight. It's twelve in the morning.

Track 25 (19.1)
Section 19.1. Learning the times of day. Listen and repeat the times of day. A.M. In the morning. 12:00AM to 11:59AM. 7:00AM. It's seven in the morning. 8:15AM. It's eight fifteen in the morning. 10:30AM. It's ten thirty in the morning. 11:45AM. It's eleven forty-five in the morning. P.M. In the afternoon. 12:01PM to 5:00PM. 12:30PM. It's twelve thirty in the afternoon. 3:45PM. It's three forty-five in the afternoon. 4:00PM. It's four o'clock in the afternoon. P.M. In the evening. 5:00PM to 9:00PM. 6:15PM. It's a quarter after six in the evening. 7:10PM. It's seven ten in the evening. 8:37PM. It's eight thirty-seven in the evening. P.M. At night. 9:00PM to 11:59PM. 9:30PM. It's nine-thirty at night. 10:15PM. It's ten fifteen at night. 11:45PM. It's a quarter to midnight.

Track 26 (19.3)
Section 19.3. Practice the short conversation with a partner. Student 1: Excuse me. What time is it? Student 2: It's three o'clock. Student 1: Thank you. Student 2: You're welcome.

Track 27 (19.4)
Section 19.4. When the time falls between :01 and :09, the proper way to say the time is by using "O" before the number. For example, for this time, you would say twelve o' one." Look at the times below and repeat. Three o' three. Eight o' one. Seven o' seven. Six o' six. Twelve o' nine. Five o' seven. Four o' eight. One o' five.

Track 28 (19.5)
Section 19.5. Conversation practice. Practice the following short conversation with a partner. Number one. A: Excuse me, can you tell me what time it is? B: Yes. It's twelve o' five. A: Thank you very much. B: You're welcome. Number two. A: Hi. Do you happen to know the time? B: Sure. It's seven o' nine. A: I appreciate it. Thank you.

Track 29 (19.6)
Section 19.6. Practice the conversation with a partner. Use "Sir" if your partner is male and "Ma'am" if your partner is female. Also, change the underlined times with 1-13. Student 1: Excuse me, sir. Do you know the time? Student 2: Yes. It's nine o' two. Student 1: Nine o' two? Wow. It's late. Thank you very much. Student 2: No problem.

Track 30 (20.2)
Section 20.2. Listen and answer the following questions. Practice with a partner and make your responses true. For example, A: Is it 5:00PM? B: No, it isn't. A: Are they students? B: Yes, they are. Number one. Is your brother in class? Number two. Is it hot outside? Number three. Is it six in the evening? Number four. Is today your birthday? Number five. Is today Monday? Number six. Are you from Africa?

Track 31 (21)
Section twenty-one. Unit two comprehension check. Listen to the conversations and answer the questions. You will hear everything two times. Number one. A: Hi. What time is it? B: It's ten o'clock. A: Thanks. What time is it? (Repeat) Number two. A: I'm really hungry. B: What time is your lunch break? A: It's at noon. What time is his lunch break? (Repeat) Number three. A: I will call you this afternoon. B: Great. What time will you call? A: At a quarter after three. When will he call? (Repeat) Number four. A: I am really tired in the morning. B: What time do you wake up? A: I wake up at 5AM. B: Well, that's why you're tired. What time does the man wake up? (Repeat) Number five. A: I eat dinner late every day. B: What time do you get home from work? A: I get home at 7:30 in the evening. B: Yeah, that is late. What time does the man get home from work? (Repeat) Number six. A: I'm late for school everyday. B: What time does school start? A: It starts at 6PM. B: Well, what time do you leave? A: I leave at a quarter to six. B: Maybe you should leave earlier. What time does he leave for school? (Repeat) Number seven. A: We better leave now. The movie starts at 7. B: What time is it now? It's 6:30. B: Yes, we better leave now. What time does the movie start? (Repeat) Number eight. A: I need to get to the store soon. B: What time does it close? A: It closes at 9PM. What time does the store close? (Repeat) Number nine. A: I want to get to the restaurant before it opens. B: What time does it open? A: It opens at 5 in the evening. What time does the

restaurant open? (Repeat) Number ten. A: Excuse me, sir. Do you have the time? B: Yes, it is ten minutes to 7. A: Ten minutes to 7? B: That's right. A: Thank you. B: You're welcome. What time is it? (Repeat)

Track 32 (22)

Section twenty-two. Days, months, seasons. Look at the words. Listen and repeat. Days of the week. Sunday. Monday. Tuesday. Wednesday. Thursday. Friday. Saturday. Months of the year. January. February. March. April. May. June. July. August. September. October. November. December.

Track 33 (22.2)

Section 22.2. Listen to the questions and write your answers. You will hear each question two times. Number one. What month is between May and July? (Repeat) Number two. What day is after Sunday? (Repeat) Number three. What month is before October? Number four. What month is after April? (Repeat) Number five. What day is between Wednesday and Friday? (Repeat) Number six. What day is before Monday? (Repeat) Number seven. What month is before August? (Repeat) Number eight. What month is between January and March? (Repeat) Number nine. What month is after November? (Repeat)

Track 34 (25)

Section twenty-five. Telling the dates. Listen and repeat. Practice with a partner. Change the meeting, date, time and locations for more practice. Pat: When do you meet for your job interview? Sam: On Thursday, March 28. Pat: What time? Sam: At 2:30 in the afternoon. Pat: Where is your meeting? Sam: At Thrift Supermarket.

Track 35 (26)

Section twenty-six. Listen and repeat the conversation. Then, students change the underlined responses with true information about themselves and practice with a partner. Student A: Hi. What days do you study English? Student B: I study English on Tuesdays and Thursdays in the evening. Student A: What times do you study English?

Track 36 (26.1)

Section 26.1. Listen to the short conversations and match the questions with the correct responses. Conversation number one. A: Hi, Jose. When is our meeting? B: Our meeting is on November thirteenth at three in the afternoon. A : What day of the week is that? A: It's on a Thursday. B: Really? That's bad for me. Listen to the conversation again. (Repeat) Question number one. What time is the meeting? Question number two. When is the meeting? Question number three. Is the meeting time good for her? Now, listen to conversation number two for questions four, five and six. A: Hello again, Jose. Listen, when is your birthday? B: My birthday is on July 26th. A: May I ask what year? B: I was born in 1971. A: Wow. This year, your birthday is on a Saturday. Listen to the conversation one more time. (Repeat) Number four. What year was Jose born in? Number five. When is his birthday? Number six. What day of the week is his birthday this year?

Track 37 (27.0)

Section 27. Unit 2 assessment. Look at the pictures and listen to the recording. Circle the correct answer A, B, or C. Number one. A: It is very cold outside. Number two. A: It's springtime! Part two. Listen and write. Listen to the conversations and answer the questions. Number one. A: Excuse me, do you know what time it is? B: Yes, it's a quarter after three. A: Thanks. Number two. A: Excuse me, I'm in a hurry. B: What's the hurry. A: It's 7 O'clock and I have to go to work. Number three. A: Hey, Hank, are you going to Maria's party this Saturday? B: Oh, it's this week? Oh man, I don't think I can go. Number four. A: Are you excited about the show this Friday? B: Yes. Yes, I am. I'm very excited! A: Me too! Number five. A: Where are you going? B: I'm on my way to the airport. My mother arrives at six in the evening.

Track 38 (28)

Section twenty-eight. Review long and short vowels. Long vowels: a, e, i, o u. Short vowels: ă, ĕ, ĭ, ŏ, ŭ.

Track 39 (28.1)

Section 28.1. Introduction to the phonetic symbol / ɜ: /. This is the sound in the world bird. Listen and repeat. Bird. Word. Heard. Third. Dirt. Learn. These words use the "er" sound. Listen and repeat. Number one. Girl. Number two. Early. Number three. Sir. Number four. Thirty. Number five. Burn. Number six. Water. Number seven. Tower. Number eight. Circle. Number nine. Finger. Number ten. Turtle. Number eleven. Feather. Number twelve. Shirt. Number thirteen. Hammer. Number fourteen. Exercise. Number fifteen. Squirrel. Number sixteen. River. Number seventeen. Mermaid. Number eighteen. Her. Number nineteen. Faster. Number twenty. Spider.

Track 40 (29)

Section twenty-nine. New vocabulary words. Ordinal numbers. Look at the words. Listen and repeat. Number one. First. Number two. Second. Number three: third. Number four. Fourth. Number five. Fifth. Number six. Sixth. Number seven. Seventh. Number eight. Eighth. Number nine. Ninth. Number ten. Tenth. Number eleven. Eleventh. Number twelve. Twelfth. Number thirteen. Thirteenth. Number fourteen. Fourteenth. Number fifteen. Fifteenth. Number sixteen. Sixteenth. Number seventeen. Seventeenth. Number eighteen. Eighteenth. Number nineteen. Nineteenth. Number twenty. Twentieth. Number twenty-one. Twenty-first. Number twenty-two. Twenty-second. Number twenty-three. Twenty-third. Number twenty-four. Twenty-fourth. Number twenty-five. Twenty-fifth. Number twenty-six. Twenty-sixth. Number twenty-seven. Twenty-seventh. Number twenty-eight. Twenty-eighth. Number twenty-nine. Twenty-ninth. Number thirty. Thirtieth. Number thirty-one. Thirty-first.

Track 41 (30)

Section thirty. The Calendar. When you say dates, the number is said as an ordinal number. For example, "The second of May" or "May second.) Practice saying the dates. Listen and repeat. July 4th. October 31st. February 14th. December 25th. May 5th. April 1st. November 21st. January 3rd. September 16th.

Track 42 (30.1)
Section 30.1. Conversation with a partner. Listen, repeat, then practice. Pat: Sam, when is your birthday? Sam: My birthday is on Thursday. Pat: What's the date on Thursday? Sam: Thursday is August 13th. Pat: August 13th? Sam: Yes, I was born on August 13th, 1990. Pat: I was also born in 1990. Sam: When is your birthday, Pat? Pat: My birthday is in December. Sam: When in December? Pat: I was born on December 2nd. Sam: That means I am older than you. Pat: Yes. You are almost four months older than me.

Track 43. (30.2)
Section 30.2. The 30 Day Song. Do you know how many days are in each month? Well, here's a fun way to remember. Sing along. 30 days has September. April, June and November. The rest have 31 days, you see, except February.

Track 44 (30.3)
Section 30.3. New vocabulary words. Important dates on the calendar. Listen and repeat. Number one. Doctor's appointment. Number two. Job interview. Number three. Dentist appointment. Number four. Rent due. Number five. Mother visits. Number six. Light bill due. Number seven. NewYear's Day. Number eight. Holiday. Number nine. Birthday party. Number ten. Concert.

Track 45 (31)
Section 31. Listen to the recordings about Eva and look at the calendar on the previous page. Circle true or false for each question. You will hear each recording two times. Number one. Eva's rent is due on Sunday, January 6th. Number two. Eva's light bill is due on January 23rd. Number three. Eva's mother visits on Friday, January 25th at 6PM. Number four. Eva's birthday party is on the 13th at 1PM. Number five. Eva's dentist appointment is on January 29th at 3:15PM.

Track 46 (32)
Section 32. Listen to the conversations and repeat. Work with a partner and reference the information from Eva's calendar. Number one. Sam: Hi Eva. I was wondering, would you have lunch with me on Thursday? Eva: Lunch on Thursday, the 17th? Sam: Yes, the 17th. Eva: Sorry, Sam. I have a doctor's appointment at that time. Sam: That's okay. Some other time, then? Eva: Sure!

Track 47 (32 continued)
Number two. Hello, Eva. I was wondering, would you have dinner with me on Friday? Eva: Dinner on Friday, the 25th? Sam: Yes, the 25th. Eva: Sorry, Sam. My other is visiting at that time. Sam: That's okay. Some other time, then? Eva: Yes, that would be nice.

Track 48 (32 continued)
Number three. Sam: How are you, Eva? I was wondering, would you have lunch with me on Monday? Eva: Lunch on Monday, the 7th? Sam: Yes, the 7th. Eva: Sorry, Sam. I have a job interview at that time. Sam: That's okay. Some other time, then? Eva: Ok!

Track 49 (32 continued)
Number four. Sam: What's up, Eva? I was wondering, would you have dinner with me on Sunday? Eva: Dinner on Sunday, the 13th? Sam: Yes, the 13th. Eva: Sorry, Sam. It's my birthday on Sunday and I am having a party. Sam: That's okay. Some other time, then? Eva: Well, why don't you come to my party? Sam: Really? I can come to your party? Eva: Yes, it will be a lot of fun. Sam: Great! See you Sunday!

Track 50 (32.3)
Section 32.3. Listen to a phone conversation and answer the questions with the correct information. Conversation one. A: Hello, doctor's office. Can I help you? B: Yes, I need to make an appointment to see Dr. Smith. A: He has an opening on January 16th at 2 PM. B: Okay. I will take that. Thank you. B: You're welcome. Listen to the conversation again. (Repeat) Number one. What doctor does the man want to see? A) Dr. Smith B) Dr. Quiñonez C) Dr. Patel. Number two. What is the date of the appointment? Number three? What time is the appointment? Conversation two. A: Hello, doctor's office. Can I help you? B: Yes, I need to cancel an appointment. A: Who is your doctor? B: Dr. Patel. A: What is the date of your appointment? B: January 17th. A: Okay. Would you like to reschedule your appointment? B: No thank you. I will call later. A: Okay. Have a nice day. Listen to the conversation again. Number one. Who is the appointment with? A) Dr. Smith B) Dr. Quiñonez C) Patel. Number two. Does the man want to reschedule the appointment? Number three. What was the date of the appointment?

Track 51 (32.5)
Section 32.5. Listen to the conversation between Paula and her doctor. Then, answer the questions. Doctor: Hi, Paula. Tell me what's wrong. Paula: Well, two days ago I started feeling sick. Doctor: Describe what you are feeling. Paula: I have a headache. I have no energy. I've been coughing a lot. And I am having trouble sleeping. Doctor: Ok. Let me listen to your heart and lungs. Breathe in deeply. That's it. Good. Well, everything sounds fine. Paula: What's wrong with me, doctor? Doctor: Most likely you have a flu. I recommend you drink lots of water and rest. Paula: Doctor, can I get a note for my boss? You know, an excuse from work? That way I can rest. Doctor: Sure. I'll write one for you now. Number one. What is wrong with Paula? A. She feels good. B. She feels sick. C. She needs work. Number two. When did she start feeling sick? A. One day ago. B. Two days ago. C. Three days ago. Number three. How does the doctor examine her? A. Checks her lungs and heart. B. Checks her eyes. C. Checks her mouth. Number four. What does the doctor say? A. You need to go to the hospital. B. Everything sounds ok. C. Everything sounds fine. Number five. What does the doctor recommend? A. Drink lots of water and rest. B. Go to work.

C. Eat lots of food. Number six. What does Paula ask for? A. Permission to return to work. B. An excuse from work. C. Permission to sleep in the doctor's office.

Track 52 (33)

Section thirty-three. Consonant blends are two or three different consonant letters put together in a word and each letter sound is heard when the word is pronounced. For example, in the word "splash," you hear the "s," the "p," and the "l" individually. Listen and repeat the following sets of words that have consonant blends.

1. (SL)	slice	sleep	8. (DR)	drag	drain	15. (TW)	twist	twelve
2. (FL)	flower	Florida	9. (TR)	trash	travel	16. (SPL)	split	splash
3. (CL)	clean	clock	10. (BL)	blanket	blue	17. (SCR)	scrape	scratch
4. (GL)	glass	glad	11. (PR)	pray	price	18. (SPR)	spread	sprinkle
5. (FR)	fry	free	12. (SP)	spend	clasp	19. (SQU)	square	squeeze
6. (BR)	broom	brain	13. (ST)	fast	stay	20. (STR)	street	straw
7. (CR)	crab	cry	14. (SW)	swing	sweep	21. (THR)	three	throw

22. (SHR) shred shrimp

The following three sets of words have consonant blends that sound like / sk /.
1.(SC) scoop screen   3. (SCH) school schedule
2. (SK) task skim

Track 53 (33.1)

Section 33.1. Listen to the following short conversation and repeat. Then, practice with a partner. A: Excuse me, where is the Florida school? B: It's on twelfth street. A: Do I need to travel very far? B: It's just about three blocks away. If you walk fast, you can get there in a few minutes. A: Thank you very much. B: Oh, you are very welcome.

Track 54 (34)

Section thirty-four. Unit 3 comprehension check. Listen to the conversations and answer the questions. You will hear each conversation two times. Number one. A: Do you work on Saturday? B: Yes, I work from 8 AM to 5 PM. What time does he work on Saturday? A) from 5PM to 8AM. B) from 5AM to 5PM. C) from 8AM to 5PM. Listen again. (Repeat) Number two. A: I have to pay my rent. B: When is your rent due? It's due on the 5th. When is his rent due? A) today. B) the 5th. C) the 6th. Listen again. (Repeat) Number three. A: I have to clean the house. Mary will be here on Sunday. B: Sunday the 11th? A: Yes, the 11th. When will Mary arrive? A) Sunday the 11th. B) Saturday the 11th. C) tomorrow. Listen again. (Repeat) Number four. A: Your car is very dirty, Manuel. You should clean your car. B: I will clean it on Thursday. When will Manuel clean his car? A) Tuesday. B) Thursday. C) today. Listen again. (Repeat) Number five. A: I need your help this afternoon. B: Sorry, I'm leaving right after lunch. A: Where are you going? B: I have to see a lawyer. I'm going to the lawyer's office. Where is he going after lunch? A) the lawyer's office. B) Manuel's house. C) work. Listen again. (Repeat) Number six. A: Do you have a dentist appointment? B: Yes, my dentist appointment is on January 29th. When is her dentist appointment? A) January 9th. B) January 19th. C) January 29th. Listen again. (Repeat) Number seven. Sam: Eva, are you busy on the 9th? Eva: Yes, I will be at a concert. Where will Eva be on the 9th? A) the dentist. B) with Sam. C) at a concert. Listen again. (Repeat) Number eight. Woman: Hey Eva. What kind of work do you do? Eva: Well, right now I'm looking for work. Woman: I heard Rosita's Restaurant is hiring. Eva: Oh? Really? I'll go there today. What is Eva looking for? A) Rosita's Restaurant. B) She's looking for work. C) She's looking for Sam. Listen again. (Repeat) Number nine. A: Hey, Tom. I was wondering. What's a good place to eat around here? Tom: Have you tried Rosita's Restaurant? A: No. What's good there? Tom: They have amazing tacos. You should go there. What is the man looking for? A) Amazing tacos. B) A place to eat. C) He's looking for Tom. Listen again. (Repeat) Number ten. Man: Hey, Kevin. How often do you play football? Kevin: If the weather is nice, I play every weekend. Man: Is it alright if I meet you out here next weekend? Kevin: Yes. And bring your friends. When does Kevin play football? A) every weekend. B) next weekend. C) outside. Listen again. (Repeat) Number eleven. A: What do you like to do on your free time? B: I like to go to the movies. A: Really? What kind of movies do you like? B: I like movies about romance. What does she like to do on her free time? A) go to the park. B) go to the movies. C) go to sleep. Listen again. (Repeat) Number twelve. A: Hey, Kevin. What are you listening to? B: A song by a band I really like. A: Really? Can I listen? [music clip] Yeah. They're good. Who are they? B: It's a band called JVMP. B: Wow. I'm downloading their music. What is the man listening to? A) a song. B) a podcast. C) a movie. Listen again. (Repeat) Number thirteen. A: Hey Steve. We're having our class party tomorrow. Are you bringing something? B: I can't make it to school tomorrow. A: Oh. That's too bad. Will Steve be at the class party tomorrow? A) Yes. B) No. Listen again. (Repeat) Number fourteen. A: I could use your help this weekend, Sam. Sam: Sorry, I have to work Saturday and Sunday. A: Okay. I understand. Thanks. Is Sam working this weekend? A) Yes. B) No. Listen again. (Repeat) Number fifteen. A: I heard it is going to snow. B: Yes. The news said it will snow tomorrow. Will it rain tomorrow? A) Yes. B) No. Listen again. (Repeat)

Track 55 (35)

Section thirty-five. Occupations. Work. There are many types of jobs. Some people work outside; some inside. Some people work at home or "remotely." These are considered indoor jobs. Here are some different kinds of occupations around the city. Which do you think are done indoors (or "inside") and which are outside? Some may be both. Listen and repeat. Number one. Plumber. Number two. Mover. Number three. Painter. Number four. Cashier. Number five. Waiter. Number six. Clinical nurse. Number seven. Solar Panel Installer. Number eight. Park Ranger. Number nine. Researcher.

Track 56 (35.1)

Sections 35.1. Indoor/outdoor jobs and identifying skills. Practice reading about each job. Point to the consonant blends, digraphs, and vowels. Listen and repeat. Number one. Plexico is a plumber. He fixes pipes. Number two. Glory is a clinical nurse. She helps sick people. Number three. Sal is a solar panel installer. He installs solar panels on houses. Number four. Shirley is a cashier. She works in a supermarket. Number five. Charley is a childcare worker. She works with little children. Number six. Raul is a researcher. He studies the environment. Number seven. Peter is a painter. He paints houses six days a week.

Number eight. Wayne is a waiter. He works in a restaurant. Number nine. Betty is a baker. She bakes cookies, cakes and bread every day.

Track 57 (37.1)
Section 37.1. Conversation practice. Turn and talk. Listen to the following conversation and repeat. Then, practice with a partner. A: When I travel to Florida, I spend a lot of time at the beach. It's great to s plash in the warm waters. B: I love Florida. I always eat lots of crabs and shrimp there. The prices aren't too expensive. A: Florida is also famous for oranges. There is nothing like fresh oranges. I squeeze them and make fresh juice. B: Fresh oranges are great, you're right. When will you travel there again? A; I will spend three weeks in Miami in November. B: Wow. You are lucky.

Track 58 (38)
Section thirty-eight. Unit three listening quiz. Look at the pictures and listen to the recordings. Match the picture that goes best with the information and circle either A, B, or C. You will hear everything two times. Part one. Number one. He's a mechanic. (Repeat) Number two. She's a hairdresser. (Repeat) Part two. Listen to the recording and answer the questions on the line. Number one. A: Can you stay for dinner? B: Well, I have to go to work. I'm driving a truck to Washington. What is the man's occupation? (Repeat) Number two. A: Hey, Manuel, what are you doing for lunch? B: I have a job interview at 12:30. When is the man's job interview? (Repeat) Number three. A: Why do you qualify for this job? B: Well, I have six years of experience. A: Wow, that's good. How many years of experience does the man have? (Repeat) Number four. A: Well, we want to hire you for the job. When can you start? B: I can start on Monday, January 14th. A: Great. See you Monday! When can the man start working? (Repeat) Number five. A: Hey, Manuel, we're having a party on Saturday. You should come to the party. B: Thank you for the invitation. But I will be working on Saturday. A: Okay. Maybe next time. What will Manuel be doing on Saturday? (Repeat) Number six. A: Hey, Manuel, I need a job. Do you know anybody that is hiring? B: Yes. Rosita's Restaurant is looking for a cook. A: Really? That's great! I will go there and apply today. What job will the man apply for? (Repeat)

Track 59 (39)
Section thirty-nine. The digraphs QU and KN. Let's begin with practicing the pronunciation of the digraphs QU and KN. Listen and repeat. Look at the pictures and practice saying the words. Number one. Quarter. Number two. Squid. Number three. Aqua. Number four. Queen. Number five. Knife. Number six. Knee. Number seven. Knob. Number eight. Knots.

Track 60 (39.1)
Section 39.1. Point to the words that have digraphs and practice repeating them. That. Love. Sing. Known. Shower. Tooth. Black. Dress. Shrimp. Quart. Cry. Quality.

Track 61 (39.2)
Section 39.2. Look at the words below. They are words with the digraphs QU and KN. Listen and repeat. KN. Number one. Knock. Number two. Kneel. Number three. Knuckle. Number four. Unknown. Number five. Knowledge. Number six. Knot. Number seven. Knockdown. Number eight. Knee. Number nine. Knob. Number ten. Knight. QU. Number eleven. Quick. Number twelve. Quart. Number thirteen. Quality. Number fourteen. Require. Number fifteen. Quiet. Number sixteen. Equipment. Number seventeen. Quit. Number eighteen. Quote. Number nineteen. Qualify. Number twenty. Quiz.

Track 62 (39.3)
Section 39.3. Practice reading sentences. Practice the sentences. Listen and repeat. Number one. The equipment is for cleaning the floors. Number two. The quality of my work is important. Number three. I fell down and hurt my knee. Number four. Knock on the door before you enter. Number five. With your experience, you qualify for the job. Number six. Mario wants to quit his job. Number seven. I will reach my quota of selling twenty cars today. Number eight. The rabbit is quick. Number nine. I will buy a quart of milk tonight. Number ten. Turn the knob and open the door.

Track 63 (39.5)
Section 39.5. Practice the conversation. Listen to the following conversation and repeat. Then, practice with a partner. Mr. Quinn: Hi Tony. I have a question. I need you to work on Saturday. Will you be available? Tony: Yes, Mr. Quinn. I will be available. What time do you need me? Mr. Quinn: I need you to come in at four in the afternoon. Tony: That's fine, Mr. Quinn. Will it be for eight hours? Mr. Quinn: Yes, eight hours. Thank you, Tony. Tony: It's quite alright.

Track 64 (39.6)
Section 39.6. More conversation practice. Listen to the short conversation and repeat. Then, practice with a partner. Ms. Knowles: I'm glad Mr. Quinn knows we will work all hours of the day. Tom: Yes, and Mr. Quinn knows we all work hard. Ms. Knowles: This is true. I think it's because we love our jobs. Tom: Yes, I agree. Ms. Knowles, do you know where the new equipment is? Ms. Knowles: New equipment? What new equipment? Tom: We have three new vacuum cleaners. Ms. Knowles: Oh, those? They are in the back of the equipment room.

Track 65 (41)
Section forty-one. Occupation tools. Identify tools used for various jobs. Number one. Wrench. Number two,. Hammer. Number three. Paint brush. Number four. Screw driver. Number five. Pliers. Number six. Ratchet. Number seven. Lawn mower. The man uses a lawn mower to cut the grass. Number eight. Shovel. The man uses a shovel to dig up dirt. Number nine. The man uses a saw to cut wood.

Track 66 (42)
Section forty-two. Unit 3 assessment. Look at the pictures and listen. Circle the correct answer. Is the correct answer A, B, or C? You will hear everything two times. Part one. Number one. She is brushing her hair. (Repeat) Number two. The store is next to the supermarket. (Repeat) Part two. Listen to the conversations. Listen again and answer the questions. You will hear everything two times. Drill one. Number one. A: Excuse me, sir. Do you have the time? B: Yes, it's

a quarter after ten. A: Thanks. Number one. What time is it? A) 10:25. B) 10:15. C) 10:45. Listen again. (Repeat) Number two. A: Can you help me today? B: I can't. I have a doctor's appointment at noon. When is the man's appointment? A) 12:00 AM. B) 12:00 PM. C) 2:00 PM. Listen again. (Repeat) Number three. Tomorrow is Friday. What day is today? A) Saturday. B) Thursday. C) Wednesday. Listen again. (Repeat) Drill two. Number four. A: What do you do at your job? B: I prepare food for customers. What is the man's occupation? A) plumber. B) waiter. C) cook. Listen again. (Repeat) Number five. A: The job requires a minimum of two years experience, Manuel. B: Well, I have four years experience. How many years of experience is required? A) two. B) four. C) six. Listen again. (Repeat) Number six. A: What do you need from the store? B: I need a quart of milk and a dozen of eggs. How much milk does the man need? A) a gallon. B) a dozen. C) a quart. Listen again. Repeat.

Track 67 (43)
Section forty-three. What are diphthongs? Diphthongs include the following pairs of letters: au, aw, ew, ow, oi, ou, and oy. There are actually two "ow" sounds. Practice the following sets of diphthongs. Listen and repeat. Number one: cow. Number two: boy. Number three: house. Number four: poison. Number five: saw. Number six: jewelry. Number seven: sauce. Number eight: bow.

Track 68 (43.1)
Section 43.1. Listen and repeat the following words with diphthongs. OW: owl, clown, town, flowers. OY: joy, toy, royal, enjoy, OU: house, mouth, pound, blouse. OI: join, soil, boil, coin. EW: few, crew, chew, screw. AW: lawn, yawn, hawk, crawl. AU: autumn, auto, fault, audio.

Track 69 (43.3)
Section 43.3. Practice the "OW" sound. The "ow" produces two sounds. One has the long o sound and the other the "ow" sound. For example, the word *know* has the long o sound, while the word *now* has the "ow" sound. Listen and repeat the words that have the long o sound. Long o: below, throw, mow, slow, show, grow, snow, borrow, bowl, elbow, follow, low, own, rows, tow, yellow. Let's practice the words that have the "ow" sound. Listen and repeat. How, now, shower, clown, plow, powder, somehow, down, towel, tower, vowel, wow, allow, bowels, crowd, brown.

Track 70 (43.4)
Section 43.4. Listen to the conversation and repeat. Then, practice with a partner. Willow: Hi, Woodrow. Do you know if it will snow tonight? Woodrow: I hope not, Willow. I don't like to plow snow. Willow: I know. It snowed 33 inches last winter. Somehow, it slows everything down. Woodrow: Wow. I didn't know that much snow fell last year. Willow: Now I hear even more is coming! Woodrow: Let's hope not too much comes down.

Track 71 (43.5)
Section 43.5. The double o makes more than one sound. One like in the word *noon*, and one like in the word *book*. Listen and repeat the words. Write them in the correct column. Room, pool, food, took, wood, too, foot, tool, balloon, soon, cook, neighborhood, look, cartoon, shook, broom, brook.

Track 72 (44)
Section forty-four. Money. Coins. Look at the different coins and their values. Listen and repeat. Number one. A Penny. One cent. Number two. A nickel. Five cents. Number three. A dime. Ten cents. Number four. A Quarter. Twenty-five cents. Number five. A half-dollar. Fifty cents. Number six. A dollar coin. One dollar.

Track 73 (44.2)
Section 44.2. Money. Bills. Look at the different dollar bills. Listen and repeat. Number one. One dollar bill. One dollar. Number two. Five dollar bill. Five dollars. Number three. Ten dollar bill. Ten dollars. Number four. Twenty dollar bill. Twenty dollars. Number five. Fifty dollar bill. Fifty dollars. Number six. One hundred dollar bill. One hundred dollars.

Track 74 (44.5)
Section 44.5. Conversation practice. Listen to the following short conversation and repeat. Then, practice with a partner. Audrey: Hi, Troy. I was wondering, how much lemonade should I bring to the party? Troy: Hello, Audrey. Well, we will have twenty people from Homestead at the party. You should bring four gallons. They love sweet lemonade. Audrey: How many people? Troy: There should be twenty people or more. Audrey: Wow. Should I bring food, too? Troy: Sure! Will you cook good food for the party? Audrey: Yes, I will. I love to cook many kinds of foods. I think I will bring grilled shrimp with a lime twist. Troy: Excellent! Everyone will enjoy that!

Track 75 (47)
Section seventy-five. Identifying clothes and colors. Look at the pictures. Listen and repeat. First, let's identify the colors. Number one: white. Number two: red. Number three: blue. Number four: yellow. Number five: brown. Number six: black. Number seven: green. Number eight: purple. Next, let's identify men's clothes. Number nine: shirt. Number ten: tie. Number eleven: belt. Number twelve: pants. Number thirteen: shoes. Number fourteen: jacket. Next, let's identify women's clothes. Number fifteen: blouse. Number sixteen: dress. Number seventeen: purse. Number eighteen: high heels. Number nineteen: glasses. Number twenty: bracelet.

Track 76 (47.1)
Section 47.1. Conversation practice. Listen to the conversation and repeat. Then, practice with a partner. Look at pictures 1, 2, and 3 and change the underlined words to make them true. A: What color is her dress? B: It's blue. A: What color are her shoes? B: They're white.

Track 77 (48)

Section forty-eight. Unit four comprehension check. Listen to the conversations and circle the answers to the questions. You will hear numbers one through four two times. Number one. A: Excuse me, sir. Are you working here? I'm looking for towels. B: Yes, towels are in the bed and bath section, and they are on sale. A: Thanks. What is the woman looking for? A) bowls. B) towers. C) towels. Listen again. (Repeat) Number two. A: I'm really thirsty. I want to buy a drink. B: There is a soda machine down the hall. They cost a .75. A: All I have is three nickels and two dimes. How much money does the man have? A) 35 cents. B) 75 cents. C) 45 cents. Listen again. (Repeat) Number three. A: I have three ten dollar bills and one twenty dollar bill. Number three. How much money does the man have? A) $30. B) $40. C) $50. Listen again. (Repeat) Number four. A: I need to buy three sandwiches for my co-workers. They gave me ten dollars to buy them. B: How much are the sandwiches? A: They are three dollars each. Number four. Does the woman have enough money for the three sandwiches? A) yes. B) no. Listen again. (Repeat) You will hear numbers five through nine one time. Number five. Which of the following sentences is in the present progressive tense? A) She eats pizza. B) She is eating pizza. C) She will eat pizza. Number six. Which of the following sentences is in the future tense? A) He will buy new shoes. B) He is buying new shoes. C) He buys new shoes. Number seven. A: I will return this shirt tomorrow. B: Why? Did your father not like it? A: He has more than five green shirts. I will change it for a purple shirt. B: That sounds like a good idea. Number seven. What color shirt does the man want to get for his father? A) green. B) purple. C) white. Number eight. A: I'm looking for a new dress. B: Will it be for the party Saturday night? A: Yes. Do you think I should buy the red dress or the blue dress? B: I think the red dress will be better. Number eight. What is the woman looking for? A) a party. B) a new dress. C) Saturday night. Number nine. A: I want to eat something healthy. B: You should eat a salad. A: But a hamburger is cheaper and I don't have a lot of money. B: Well, if you want something healthy, you should buy the salad instead of the hamburger. Number nine. What does the man want to eat? A) something healthy. B) a hamburger. C) something cheaper.

Track 78 (50)

Section fifty. Safety signs. Signs have important information. They can give directions or tell us something is dangerous. Look at the signs below. Listen and repeat. Number one. Do not enter. Number two. Caution. Wear safety goggles when using equipment. Number three. Danger. Poison. Number four. Flammable. Number five. Emergency exit. Number six. High voltage. Number seven. No smoking. Number eight. Caution. Wet floor. Number nine. First aid.

Track 79 (50.3)

Section 50.3. Listen to the short conversations. Then match the safety sign that goes with each conversation and circle either A, B, or C. You will hear everything two time. Number one. Which sign are the men talking about? A: Do you know where to enter this place? B: Yes, over there. Number one. Which sign are the men talking about? Number two. Which sign are the women talking about? A: Look! We are too late. B: We'll have to come back tomorrow. Number two. Which sign are the women talking about?

Track 80 (51)

Section fifty-one. Unit four assessment. Look at the pictures and listen. Circle the correct answer. Is the correct answer A, B, or C? You will hear everything two times. Part one. Number one. A: The woman is buying new shoes. (Repeat) Number two. A: Be careful. The floor is wet. (Repeat) Part two. Listen to the conversations. Listen again and answer the questions. You will hear everything two times. Drill one. Number one. A: I am buying four bananas for one dollar. Number one. How much is each banana? A) 20 cents. B) 25 cents. C) 30 cents. (Repeat) Number two. A: I counted fifty men and fifty women in the restaurant. B: Wow. That's a lot of people. Number two. How many people are in the restaurant? A) 100 people. B) 50 people. C) 200 people. (Repeat) Number three. A: I am trying to eat healthy. B: How are you going to do that? A: I like pizza, but I am going to buy a salad instead. Also, I am drinking water instead of soda. Number three. Which food is healthy? A) Soda. B) Pizza. C) Water. (Repeat) Drill two. Number four. A: It's the first day of the year and everyone is celebrating! Number four. What holiday is it? A) St. Patrick's Day. B) Valentine's Day. C) New Year's Day. (Repeat) Number five. A: Which one is the new teacher? B) Oh, he's the one wearing the blue shirt and black tie. A: Thanks. Number five. What is the new teacher wearing? A) a blue tie and shirt. B) a blue shirt and black tie. C) a black shirt and blue tie. (Repeat) Number six. A: Will you help me right now? B: I can't. I'm mowing the lawn. Number six. What is the man doing? A) Plowing snow. B) mowing the lawn. C) tying a bow. (Repeat)

CREDITS AND ACKNOWLEDGEMENTS

The author would like to give a special THANKS to the following people for this second edition: Yancy Diaz, Schuyler Torres, Antonios Hatzigeorgalis, Adrian Utley, Sam Shepard, Lauren Katauskas, Barbara Williams, Sherri Alman, Khatereh Plesnik, Harry Preston, Abdul Sesay, Irene LeRoy, and Steve Fisher.

Voice over contributors include: Jose V. Torres, Toyin Fadiran, Jennifer Folayan, Sam Shepard, Megan Koterba, Liz Metzger, Schuyler Torres, and Charlie Emerson.

Music on the audio tracks composed by: Jose V. Torres and JVMP, except "Funky Boxstep" and "Arroz Con Pollo" by Kevin MacLeod (incompetech.com), and "30 Day Song" performed by Pat Renny Alzadon. Download the music of JVMP at jvmp.bandcamp.com. Some music tracks licensed by Envato.

Layout design by: Jose V. Torres
Cover photo by: Ricardo CL
Cover design by @create_shema

Licensing and permission for illustrations, vectors and photos provided by: Graphic Stock (graphicstock.com), Adobe, Envato, Pixabay, Pexels (pexels.com) and Open Clip Art (openclipart.org).

Logo redesign by: Jose V. Torres

Subscribe to our YouTube channel at YouTube.com/JoseTorresiwtle

All audio tracks are available for free at iwtle.com/2-2/audio2

ABOUT THE AUTHOR

Jose Vasilio Torres is a teacher with over 20 years of experience working with English Learners from the middle school grades to adults. Torres began his career in the English program at Miami Dade College in Miami, Florida. He subsequently relocated to Baltimore, Maryland where he worked with several adult English learner programs, as well as working in public schools. Torres first published "I Want To Learn English" in 2016 with a grant from the Maryland TESOL organization and presented his research associated with the textbook at the TESOL International Conference in Seattle, Washington the following year. Torres also presented his research findings at the LESLLA (Literacy Education and Second Language Learning for Adults) 13th Symposium in 2017.

Jose V. Torres at the screening of his film "The Beggar" at the Ocean City Film Festival in 2022. Photo by Yancy Diaz.

Torres earned his B.A. in English from Florida International University in Miami, Florida and his Master's in TESOL from Notre Dame of Maryland University in Baltimore, Maryland. He began doing his research and collecting data for this textbook in 2011 as a project. Later, he began the first trials of Units 1 and 2 while working at Baltimore City Community College. By 2014, a nearly complete book was tried for multiple classes with the help of other instructors at the BCCC program. Students' made immediate and significant gains on their test scores. Torres devoted 2015 to completing the textbook and publishing it so other instructors around the United States and other countries could share this very effective English language methodology with their students. What has resulted has been a very successful usage of the *I Want To Learn English* methodology. Now, Torres has taken things to a whole new level, incorporating video to give English learners even more options.

Have a question or comment for the author? Send him an email. You can reach Jose at **iwanttolearnenglish3@gmail.com**.

I WANT TO LEARN ENGLISH

LANGUAGE SKILLS FOR THE REAL WORLD

This textbook was especially designed as a comprehensive, interactive resource tool to teach English learners at a beginner proficiency level. Its proven effectiveness makes it an ideal choice for schools, refugee programs, and English learning centers across the United States and in countries around the world. Its practice, real world uses infuses contextualization with high frequency vocabulary and phonetic components. This combination gives English and Multi-language learners the most productive English language experience available in a very affordable textbook.

Audio and video components accompany this textbook.

Improve Comprehension

Build Phonemic Awareness

www.iwtle.com